Creating Success
from the
Inside Out

Creating Success
from the
Inside Out

DEVELOP THE FOCUS
AND STRATEGY
TO UNCOVER THE
LIFE YOU WANT

EPHREN W. TAYLOR II
with
W. EMERSON BRANTLEY III

BICENTENNIAL
1807
WILEY
2007
BICENTENNIAL

John Wiley & Sons, Inc.

Published by John Wiley & Sons, Inc., Hoboken, New Jersey.
Published simultaneously in Canada.

Wiley Bicentennial Logo: Richard J. Pacifico

For general information on our other products and services or for technical support, please contact our Customer Care Department within the United States at (800) 762-2974, outside the United States at (317) 572-3993 or fax (317) 572-4002.

Wiley also publishes its books in a variety of electronic formats. Some content that appears in print may not be available in electronic books. For more information about Wiley products, visit our web site at www.wiley.com.

Library of Congress Cataloging-in-Publication Data:

Taylor, Ephren W. (Ephren White), 1982–
    Creating success from the inside out : develop the focus and strategy to uncover the life you want / Ephren W. Taylor.
        p.   cm.
    ISBN 978-0-470-17713-6 (cloth)
        1. Success in business—Psychological aspects.   2. Entrepreneurship—Psychological aspects.   3. Investments—Social aspects.   4. Humanitarianism.   5. African American businesspeople—Biography.   I. Title.
    HF5386.T3195   2008
    650.1—dc22
                                                        2007026268

Printed in the United States of America.

10   9   8   7   6   5   4   3   2   1

This book is dedicated to my loving wife and number one supporter MeShelle Taylor, my two wonderful children Ephren and Madison, and my parents Ephren and Diane Taylor, whose encouragement, guidance, and love helped me to find my own path to success. A special thanks is due to our church family at the Johnson County Church of Christ, who loved us before and after our successes; when we had little and when we were blessed with plenty. And to the City Capital Team and to all those who have supported, invested, encouraged, mentored, and loved us along this road, may all the work we do continue to bring glory unto His name.

Contents

Section III The Dark Hall of Fear 89

Section IV Empowerment versus Victimhood 117

Section V Why Every Young Person Should Start a Business 151

Section VI Getting What You Need to Succeed 179

Section VII   Don't Listen to Losers, Whiners, and Naysayers—Believe in Yourself   223

Preface

W. Emerson Brantley III

In October 2005 I received an e-mail from somebody who'd developed a real estate concept and wanted me to help him market the concept. That wasn't that remarkable, but 15 minutes later a second e-mail popped up from the same sender. He told me a little more about who he was and what he had accomplished, and finished by saying he wanted to retain me for the next 15 months to create a national marketing program. What made this e-mail especially unique was that I had never spoken to, or communicated with this individual before, yet there it was: "I'd like to retain you through the end of 2006." This caught my attention. I wanted to talk to this guy. He was either crazy, or trying to impress with his audacity . . . or he was an incredibly intuitive and decisive individual.

Within the first 10 minutes of our first call, I knew he wasn't crazy, and he wasn't trying to impress me . . . but he was extremely intuitive and decisive. He was very articulate about his goals and showed a higher level of business acumen than many multimillionaires I've known and worked with over the past 30 years. And he was also one of the most genuine people I had ever talked with in my entire marketing career.

Ephren was black and had just turned 23, I was white and 48. None of that mattered to him, or to me. Based solely on his visit to my web site, Ephren Taylor felt I was the person he wanted, and had made a business decision to retain me. Extraordinary qualities for someone about the same age as my daughters. I saw immediately the potential of his vision, and more importantly, that here was a man who would commit the effort, find the funding, and do whatever else it took to reach his goals. Extraordinary. I signed on, and within a few short months "fired" other long-term marketing clients to come onto the board and into the company.

So what makes Ephren Taylor tick? By almost any yardstick you care to use, Ephren Taylor is an unqualified success. He started his first successful company, Flame Software, at age 12 to develop 3D video games. At 16, Ephren won the Teen TechFest Challenge, sponsored by Microsoft, and used $1,000 savings to start a job search engine for teens. He then won a scholarship from the Kauffman Center for Entrepreneurial Leadership that allowed him to develop and hone his business skills. He personally raised over $250,000 in private funding and his web site grew into the highly successful GoFerretGo.com, ranked by *YoungBiz* magazine as number 4 of the "100 Top Companies Run by Teens" nationwide.

Ephren then turned his attention toward creating profitable investments for churches. Using his father's church as a model, he began investing their endowment monies into the community around them, originally in pretty conventional real estate rehabs. He earned returns that in some cases matched a decade of money market or bank interest on church accounts. He was 19.

He began speaking at churches, teaching stewardship, financial concepts, and more, helping them learn to grow their money within the community by giving rather than taking. Congregations would give their money or use their credit so their church could purchase a property and earn cash flow and equity. Several civic leaders in various cities took notice and began to offer him surplus properties that needed rehabbing for urban families, homes other investors were passing up in favor of big dollar developments. About the same time, people began to say, "I like using my money and credit to help my church, but can I get some of those returns for my retirement account, too?" That was the beginning of the investment programs that continue to be developed in today's City Capital Corporation.

Expanding on these concepts, four short years later, in the spring of 2006, Ephren became CEO of a multimillion-dollar public corporation: (City Capital Corporation: CCCN) with business interests throughout the United States and overseas. At age 23, he is the youngest African American CEO of any public company in history. He has earned a wall full of accolades and recognitions including State Champion and then National Champion of the Future Business Leaders of America in 1999, and Kansas Entrepreneur of the Year award in 2002. He has been asked to serve on national panels on housing issues, financial self-sufficiency within urban communities, national market conditions.

Ephren Taylor has an aggressive, proactive approach to everything he does and believes in surrounding himself with extremely high-quality individuals to form a strong team, to make the vision a reality. Today that team represents over 225 years of expertise in finance, marketing, development, management, and much more.

As of the writing of this book, Ephren Taylor is still only 24, yet his companies manage millions of dollars in assets including biofuels research, community development, and investment programs.

City Capital's mission of **"Socially-Conscious Investing to Empower Urban Communities,"** which originally focused on providing affordable homes for working class families, now has expanded its vision to include renewable resources and empowering people in other nations as well. While the company is a for-profit corporation, its roots are in the charitable sector, and it continues to plow significant portions of corporate profits back into local communities, in some cases as much as 40 percent. City Capital does this through partnerships with local, state and federal governments, community organizations, churches, and colleges.

Ephren Taylor's story, and his companies' socially conscious agenda, have made him extremely attractive to local and national media. He is often invited as a guest expert on hundreds of local and national television and radio shows including CNBC's *Big Idea*, Tom Joyner's morning show on Fox News *Bulls & Bears*, and many more. He has served as keynote speaker for dozens of colleges and business organizations, and is regularly asked to address prestigious groups such as the Wall Street Economic Summit and the Congressional Black Caucus and others.

He never completed college, yet he is in top demand as a speaker in college business classes, high schools, Boys and Girls Clubs, and other youth organizations nationwide. Ephren Taylor has spoken before tens of thousands of all ages; from large auditoriums at national conventions, to small classrooms of children and teens, to national panels on housing and economic growth in our nation's capital and on Wall Street.

Ephren Taylor has spearheaded private summits that have included investors, boards of directors of major corporations, economic development group committees, government and community leaders, and even heads of state. His Urban Wealth Tour will visit 15 cities in 2007, where he will present his economic empowerment message to hundreds of thousands across America, and bring together educational, nonprofit, and government forces to create positive change in urban communities.

In April 2007, Ephren presented the largest donation ever to Cheyney University, the oldest historically black university in America, establishing the Ephren W. Taylor II Entrepreneurship Academy to bring real-world entrepreneurial skills to urban youth.

Ephren Taylor is especially interested in reaching young men and women and helping them find their own keys to success. For these, our future leaders, business owners, and employees, as well as those of us already in the business world, he offers this collection of the thoughts and insights that have driven this world-class entrepreneur and businessman.

Though still a young man, Ephren Taylor is a person who is admired and respected throughout the business community. Yet, what sets Taylor apart from most wealthy and successful businesspeople is his fierce commitment to improving communities and enhancing the lives of the less fortunate. Giving back to the community and supporting charitable projects is as much a part of his business plan as the quarterly profit and loss statements. In fact, those who know him best would say that this focus, backed by his deep faith and conviction, is how Ephren Taylor is *"Creating Success from the Inside Out."*

Introduction

Who Am I, and Why Should You Care about What I Have to Share?

There are really two introductions in order: one for this book, and one for me. I realize most Americans have never heard of me, and that's okay because you have now! I've been working since I was 12, not for publicity or fame, but to build businesses; businesses that have been successful, profitable, and have improved peoples' lives. This book shares the business and life philosophies I've developed along the way, and have repeatedly proven to be true in my own life. Principles that will change your life, if you're up to the challenge, and help you reach your goals.

Different people will find different areas of inspiration and education here. Your background will have a direct effect on how much this book influences you because we filter everything through our mind and our life experiences. I have learned that, in the end, **our perceptions truly are our reality.** I would like you to think about this for a few moments before going on. We'll talk more about it later, but right now ask yourself, "How have my perceptions created the realities of my life up until now, and how are they filtering everything around me today?"

So, who am I to be telling you all of this? I'm just a man. And a young man at that. I'm Ephren White Taylor II. I'm the son of Ephren Taylor Sr. and Diane Taylor. I'm the brother of Marcquest and Kedron Taylor, my two brothers, each of us four years apart. I'm the husband of MeShelle Taylor. And I'm the father of Ephren III and Madison Elise Taylor. As this book is being written, I've just turned 24.

People have called me a lot of things over the years: Dumb kid, nerd, dreamer, wunderkind, genius, smart guy, lucky. I've been given nicknames by the media such as "E-Money" and "E-Billions." I've been referred to as a wealth engineer, activist mogul, a "high-performance visionary with the ability to make things happen, when nobody else can," "the Warren Buffett of the hip hop generation," and "Living Black History," among many others. I've also been accused of not being "authentic" or "genuine" because of my successes, like being black and smart or successful is somehow not "keeping it real." I've had my share of some other names that have been pretty derogatory, but I tend to let most of those roll off my back. I also don't let all this praise affect me or go to my head.

I've been a preacher, a teacher, an entrepreneur, a business owner, a CEO, and a chairman, a fundraiser, a developer, a public speaker, and more. I've been featured as a guest panelist and keynote speaker for conferences, and appeared on countless radio and television broadcasts nationwide. Hundreds of magazine and newspaper articles, maybe thousands by now, have been written about me and my meteoric rise in the business world, not to mention tens of thousands of Web page articles.

Since about age 19, most of my focus, and that of my companies, has been on connecting individuals, corporations, and churches to wealth. I have clients in Wall Street boardrooms; in South Central Los Angeles; in Anchorage, Alaska; Wichita, Kansas; Macon, Georgia; and in other cities and towns all across the United States. I've worked closely with Hip Hop icons such as Snoop Dogg and others. Along the way, I've made—and lost—millions of dollars, and I've helped change the face of entire communities.

Why Business?

I figured out pretty early that I couldn't dance too well, I couldn't hold a note to sing, and even though I was pretty good at football, a diagnosis of scoliosis ended my chances of becoming an NFL pro.

For most black teenagers, that pretty much eliminates all the obvious legal options to make it big.

But I didn't buy into the notion that I had to do any of those things to succeed. **I refused to be a victim.** I didn't want to go to work for someone else, and I wasn't raised to think that the government owed me or my family anything. Because of my incredible parents, I knew I could achieve whatever I set my sights on, and I didn't listen to the clowns, the politicians, and the media personalities who tried to tell me anything different.

Motivational speakers like to say, "If I can do it, you can do it, too!" There's a lot of truth in that. The real core, the part that's often missed, is that while we may be able to do pretty much *anything* we set our minds to, consciously or subconsciously *we choose not to do most things*, including those that will lead us to success in life. In this book, I'll prove this to you: our minds literally keep us from success. Or make it all possible.

Sometimes these choices are simply our preferences, like I never wanted to flip hamburgers for a living. Other times there is something inside us that keeps us back, and that something—the things we like to avoid within ourselves—is what keeps success just outside our grasp.

> *True success begins when we simply find that inner spark, that talent, that passion in our lives, and go after it to the exclusion of all the other things.*

God gave us all a living spirit, one in his likeness. He didn't create junk, or make you superior or inferior to anyone else. He did, however, give us certain talents. It's up to us to make up our minds to use the talents we have, and go for it!

A Disclaimer

Before we get into this any more, I want to be really clear about one point: I'm not here to give you a "How-To" guide to riches and fame. Anybody who tries to offer you his or her step-by-step "E-Z Guide" to achieving wealth is usually selling something of little value. In fact, the value is almost the inverse of the cost of the information: in other words, the more expensive the course, the less real-world value it often has.

On the other hand, there are loads of real information resources available, most of them inexpensive or even free. Napoleon Hill's *Think and Grow Rich*, Conrad Hilton's *Be My Guest*, Michael Gerber's *The E-Myth*, former GM head Alfred Sloan's book, *My Years with General Motors*, Kenneth Blanchard's *The One Minute Manager*, Collins and Porras *Good to Great*, and Dan Peña's *Building Your Own Guthrie* are just a few examples. If I were teaching a college course on success, I'd make them all required reading. One more I rely on constantly is the *Bible*. In it I've found the true keys to success, which are all based on *giving*. It has never failed to give me the guidance I've needed, even through some of the roughest, bleakest times I've faced.

I've found the Bible to be an incredible "user's manual" in my life. For example, in "I Samuel," this kid David had to take lunch to his brothers. He was around 14 or so, and had acne. (Yeah, I know, you never knew the Bible talked about stuff like that!) His brothers were soldiers, and they happened to be in a standoff with the giant, Goliath. David hears the soldiers talking about what the person gets who kills Goliath, and he was blown away. King Saul was giving away money, his daughter's hand in marriage . . . he'd even eliminate the champion's taxes for life. David jumps in and asks them to repeat the prizes, "WHAT!? What does the man get who kills the giant?" But his brothers get angry and tell him to go back to his sheep. Go home! Get outta here! This stuff ain't for kids!

The next moment is so rich, so real. I think of it every time I get dissed or someone tells me I can't do something. All the Bible says is, **"And he turned from him to another . . ."** Wow. Just like that. He didn't listen to those clowns . . . he just tuned them out and kept his eyes on the prize. He turned away and ignored them, and asked someone else for the information he needed. And you know the rest of the story.

So many times in our lives we are willing to listen to all the voices telling us why we "can't" do something. Why we're not smart enough, fast enough, rich enough, or whatever. We listen to all the Conventional Wisdom about how our age, or our race, or gender is a handicap. And more often than not the first key step toward our dreams hinges on this one moment: **Do we listen? Or do we turn from them to another?** I've done both. In every case, the turning away from the negative and toward my dreams and goals *always* led me to the information and resources I needed to succeed.

As we'll see, however, just having the right knowledge, experience, and other resources in your hands isn't enough. If it were that simple, everybody would be living in mansions on Easy Street driving BMWs and Hummers. There are other steps and strategies to keep us on track to success. If you'll let me, I'd like to spend the next few pages sharing my insights into "what true success is," and some of my life experiences, as well as some specific ways to get your mind—and your life—aimed in the right direction. And then, how to follow through and stay on track until you reach your own dreams and goals in life.

What Makes Someone a Success?

First, let's talk about what you see as success and what I see as success. I find this is easier by first looking at the things I DON'T consider success, despite Conventional Wisdom (which as we'll see is almost always wrong anyway). To me it isn't wearing certain clothes, reading the right books, or going to a certain school that lifts a man or woman up in the world, it's his or her way of thinking. Many young people lose sight of this. They think that if they just had a cool car and a great house, everything would work out great and they'd have the kind of respect they deserve. Maybe if they had a brand new pair of $200 sneakers or a lot of gold and platinum bling to show off, they'd be on top of the world.

So they set off pursuing these things—begging, borrowing, stealing, whatever—and no matter how many things they're able to collect, sooner or later they discover that *things* are not the answer. They are empty goals. Even when you get them, *if* you get them, you really have nothing. And often, after all their efforts *getting*, many people lose it all anyway. For some, that's what it takes to understand that it's not stuff that makes us somebody. It's the giving we do more than the getting. And some people never get it.

To me, your way of thinking is what ultimately makes you successful in life. That eight inches between your ears is all the ammunition, motivation, and creativity you need to make it. It controls whether you are a giver, or a taker; someone who's out for Number One only, or someone who's a team builder. What I would like to do is give you an idea of how I think and how other successful people think.

The way I look at it is this: I can't give you the road map for your life, but I can sure give you a compass and some powerful travel tips. A compass can't tell you which road to take but it will always tell you if you're headed in the right direction. And having a guide, someone who's been there, done that before you is always a big help. But ultimately, acting on the information and using the compass is all up to us, individually. Fair enough?

SECTION

Begin Where You Are Now

Robert Schuller famously said, "Bloom where you are planted!" You have to start where you are right now, not where you'd like to be or where you think you will be whenever, but right now. We have no promises about tomorrow, and we've already lost every minute in our life up until now. Even spiritually speaking, we are told, "Today is the day of salvation." Well, today is the day to start following your dream, too.

I wasn't born rich and I didn't inherit wealth. I didn't begin life as some super-successful business mogul. My family wasn't wealthy, but I grew where I was planted. We don't get to pick things like who our parents are or where we're born, but we do get to decide what we do with what we have been given to work with.

Two Parents and True Commitment

When I started out, I probably wasn't much different from you. I wasn't a dummy, but trust me, I was no Einstein, either. In high school I averaged a 2.9 GPA. Even though my family wasn't well-to-do, I did have the advantage of growing up in a loving and supportive two-parent household. I had loving parents who raised me to believe in myself, and in my own abilities to accomplish whatever I set out to do. If you also had this advantage but you don't appreciate the value of it, this next section is for you. If you feel you were handicapped because you didn't have a positive childhood or uplifting parenting, or you came from a broken home, there's a good lesson for you as well.

We all have certain strengths and weaknesses, but coming from a single-parent home almost always creates a more difficult path through life. You don't have to believe this if you don't want to, but the facts are so overwhelming they can't be ignored. In this section, you'll see clearly, perhaps for the first time, what you need to do to overcome the parental decisions that created that broken home, and how to break the cycle for your children as well. Your legacy is the thing that really matters, and after achieving your own success, it becomes almost *all* that matters.

I was born in Port Gibson, Mississippi, the son of Ephren Taylor Sr. and Diane Taylor. I was the oldest of three brothers. When I was born, we lived in my grandmother's house in Carlisle, Mississippi. It sat up on cinder blocks and had a tin roof and no hot water. That only lasted about a year. My dad had gotten an honorable discharge from the army and was working on a two-year degree at the local junior college. His father had died when Dad was only 12, but he remembered how Granddad had repeatedly told him, "Go to school, get a job! Go to school, get a job!" So that's what he did. My father was not an entrepreneur. When he graduated, he hooked up with an engineering company that contracted with nuclear power plants around the country. Dad's new job meant big changes in our lives in a lot of ways.

Dad landed a job in Homestead, Florida, so we moved to an apartment there. By the time my brothers came along, we were living in pretty decent houses in pretty decent neighborhoods. All the while, Dad kept plugging away at his electrical engineering degree. It took him 10 years to get his bachelor's degree, mixing and matching course credits at different schools, wherever we happened to live at the time. Dad's job caused us to move around a lot, and before sixth grade we had moved from Homestead to Plymouth, Massachusetts; Decatur, Alabama; Evans, Georgia; back to Decatur; and finally to Overland Park, Kansas, a suburb of Kansas City. He eventually finished his master's degree in Overland Park, and began working in the main office in Kansas City instead of out in the field in the actual nuclear power plants.

I don't remember much from each of those places because early childhood memories all kind of fuzz together. I just remember I was the new kid in school a lot, and a shyness crept in that could have taken over my life if God hadn't been at work. I was about halfway through sixth grade when we moved to Kansas. Overland Park is located in Johnson County, the second wealthiest county in the country. In 2007, *Money* magazine ranked Overland Park the sixth best city to live in the United States. I had no idea how important all this would be in my life. The quality of education I received, and the community and lifestyle I became a part of, elevated me in so many ways. But it sure didn't seem that way my first day in school in Overland Park.

There's no way of telling my story without touching on race issues as part of it. I don't focus on it or even think about it much, but from the time I was in school, I've been aware that I was different. Not just black, but unique in other ways, too. Most kids don't want to be unique, they don't want to stand out from the crowd too much. They want to be accepted by their peers. Kids want to fit in, especially when they're moving every year or so to a new school. I was the same way.

When I was in Alabama, I was in the gifted program. When we moved to Overland Park and I started middle school, they never even tested me. My parents chose to send me to the Blue Valley School District, which is in a predominately white suburb. I guess the counselors figured, "Black kid, Alabama . . . regular classes." They never did put me back into the gifted program. Yet now they have my posters at the school and all that, and colleges and high schools around the country are standing in line for me to come "inspire" their students. So did I let it hold me back? Use it as some kind of excuse or grudge? No.

I tell people it's sort of like Thomas Edison, whose teacher thought he was "addled" and so he only had three months of school. Guess he didn't care much for excuses, either!

Anyway, the first day at this clean little white suburban school all the kids were asking me, "Can you play basketball? Do you play basketball?" It's like, is that all black kids are supposed to do? Play basketball? I did play football, but nobody asked that. I'm thinking, what is wrong with these kids? They'd ask me other weird stuff like, "How does your hair stay there?" As dumb as some of the questions were, I realized they were just ignorant kids who'd never been around many African Americans before.

The worst thing of all was that there were only seven black kids total, in the whole school. And I was the only "black nerd." So, even with the other black kids—in some cases, *especially* with the other black kids—I was hard up against some of the worst black stereotypes that exist within the black community. These are stereotypes that equate to "authentic blackness," and "knowing your roots," "keepin' it real," and the kinds of things that keep people in lives of mediocrity.

Anyway, as far as the school was concerned, I wasn't considered gifted or technically any smarter than the other kids in the school. My grades dropped to around 2.9 GPA largely because I was bored, but I know too that part of it was that "not sticking out" thing. Looking back it's funny because I was already "sticking out" and didn't realize how much! I was already working on my first company, Flame Software. But at the time, I just wanted a different video game to play because I had already top-leveled-out on the couple of game cartridges I had.

Fortunately, at home I never had those kinds of problems. My life at home promoted self-awareness, excellence, and brains. My parents had no issues with their "blackness" or "being authentic" or anything like that.

> *The most important advantage I had growing up was*
> *something I never really thought too much about.*
> *Something that for me was just part of normal life.*

As difficult as it may be for many to accept, growing up in a two-parent home with a stay-at-home mom and a dad who came home from work every night was the one major advantage I had over many of my classmates. My mom had stopped working outside the home and stayed home with me when I was real small. She was there for all of us, including my two brothers—Marcquest, who came along when I was four, and Kedron four years later.

My home life was pretty normal. I figured it was a typical household, like all kids do. Only years later would I realize how fortunate I was. For instance, Mom was a stickler about dinner. Dinner was at 5:30 every day and we all ate together. My dad got off at 5 and Mom had dinner on the table when he walked in the door. We didn't dare miss dinner. I figured every family did breakfast and dinner together, and lunch too, on weekends.

Having Mom's influence at home really takes us right to the point: When do most teenagers get in trouble? When do most teenage pregnancies happen? Between the hours of 3:00 PM and 6:00 PM, when they're out of school with no one around to supervise, no one around to care. There are pretty dramatic differences between the way I was brought up and the way my wife MeShelle was raised. I had two happily married parents . . . and *still* have two happily married parents. There was no domestic violence, and both were very, very good role models.

I'm not pretending it was all like some TV family, but it was a very secure, loving environment. My wife grew up with parents who had separated. When you're a kid, you only know what you know. Living in a broken home creates all sorts of emotional baggage to wrestle with, especially issues of fear and trust. On the other hand, when you come out of a household with two loving parents, you have an invaluable head start in life right off the bat, despite whatever other negative influences outside of the household pull at you.

Now someone may say, "But what if you have a two-parent home where there's strife and abuse? Surely a single-parent home with love is better than that!" That's a hard question, and there is no reason why any person—man, woman, or child—should have to stay in an abusive situation. But my point isn't to debate the "whys" that may or may not justify a broken home. Regardless of the reason that created it, a single-parent home has distinct disadvantages when it comes to creating the environment that fosters success. I know of no study that has ever disputed this, and sadly, roughly half of the children in America are living in this reality.

MeShelle

I've already mentioned my wife's experience. She grew up in the inner city of Kansas City, Missouri. MeShelle had two older sisters. There was violence in the home, but her parents kept most of their problems out of sight of the kids, especially MeShelle, the baby. MeShelle was an exceptional kid by anyone's standards. Before she was one year old, she would fuss until her mom dressed her up all pretty before her daddy got home. She showed all sorts of talent for music and dance, well before she was in kindergarten. Fortunately, her parents saw her potential and enrolled her in special classes to encourage it.

By the time MeShelle was nine, her parents were separated. She saw her father only on weekends and holidays. He had a separate life, with a separate family. Seeing your father on weekends is better than having a father who abandons you, but all that doesn't matter when you're a kid and you scrape your knee. Mom's there to kiss it, but you want Daddy to, too. By the time you see Daddy the next weekend, it's all healed, and it's just not the same. When you ace a test, telling him over the phone isn't as good as if he was right there.

Her mom Marcy was there to support her daughters. Marcy struggled sometimes working three jobs, but always managed to earn enough to keep her daughters in clothes and food, and the mortgage paid. Eventually she turned to gambling on the nearby riverboats to supplement her meager salary. Sometimes she would earn more on a single night than her month's pay. But she realized increasingly, as she looked at the losers straggling off in the early morning hours, that she was looking at herself, if she kept on that path.

Marcy turned her back on gambling, stopped looking for the easy way out, and put herself back on a solid financial track. She was determined to make sure MeShelle knew how to carry herself and be a lady, so Marcy put MeShelle through her own "School of Etiquette," as she called it. It sure paid off!

The first time I saw MeShelle, I saw this polished young woman, never knowing the scars of her background or what she had over-come in her life up to that point. I first met her when I tagged along with a friend to a roller skating rink, and saw MeShelle gliding around the floor. We met and talked, and talked.

Pretty soon I figured out she was the one for me. The first time I went to pick her up, her mom eyed me up and down and said, "What do you think you're looking for, coming over to the hood for my daughter?" I guess I passed the test because she accepted that I was interested in her daughter for real.

I give a lot of credit to her mom's commitment to let MeShelle develop her inner talents, at considerable expense. It's not a path many inner city, single moms can afford, or take time to develop in their kids.

At one point, Marcy had to make the tough choice to take MeShelle out of a primarily black dance school because she felt they were holding her daughter back. She anguished over the decision, eventually enrolling MeShelle in a dance school that was primarily white, where there was more exposure to the art, and additional opportunities for her competitively.

MeShelle was really fortunate. After growing up in a single-parent home, MeShelle is doubly committed to working with me to keep our home together. (Which isn't always easy, especially with the kind of schedule I keep!) And she shares with other young people and couples from her own experiences, about the value of commitment to each other, and to providing that quality of environment for our family.

A Different Story

Unfortunately, the statistics tell a different story for most of these kids. Numbers show that 68 percent of black kids have only one parent: their mother. Oh, various men may come and go, or their mom may have a relationship with just one man, but the kid doesn't see them married. They don't see, and often don't feel, the commitment from the odd partner in the deal. Not just from him to their mom, but to them and to their brothers and sisters as well. He's not their "dad," and no matter how good a man he is, the expectation is that one day he'll leave them, abandon them, just like their own father and the others along the way.

There Are More than Just Emotional Disadvantages

Thirty-five percent of single-parent families are living under the poverty level, *twice as many* as those who are living with two married parents. This means less money for extracurricular activities, for training, for courses, or even for books—less money to help the children financially when they're starting out on their own, to give them a cushion. Every penny goes to basic living expenses. This is an incredibly negative financial change over the last 40 or 50 years. Seventy-eight percent of young people got married in the 1950s. Not only is staying married better from a social viewpoint, it's better in an economic sense. Marriage is almost like its own investment: It's practically a wealth-creating institution. *A married man earns from 10 percent to over 40 percent more than a single man.*

The Results from All This Is Out There, and It's Not Good

Is it too big a leap to recognize that broken families also lead to kids and adults who get in trouble with the law? Actually it's been proven many times over. In fact, it's been called pandemic, or a "corrosive epidemic," all across the United States. You may have heard the reports that today there are more black men in jail and prison than in college. This is true, but if you only count the ones in prison that are 18 to 24 years old, there are actually more in college than prison. Either way, black men have still had major reverses over the past generation or so. I'm talking about the generation I was born in. In 1980, African American college men outnumbered those imprisoned (of all ages) by over a quarter million. But by 2000, it was almost reverse: there were over 188,000 more incarcerated black men (18–55+ years old) than those in higher education.

The 2001 statistics show that when we just look at black men 18 to 24 years old in college versus those in jail or prison, it runs 2.6 to 1. In other words, when we limit it to those ages alone, you've got more black males in college than jail. Sounds a lot better, doesn't it? But when you look at white males in the same group, the ratio is 28 to 1. Twenty-eight times more white men are in college than prison. That's 10 times the ratio for black males (U.S. Department of Justice data).

People can argue over whether it paints a clearer picture looking at just the narrower age ranges, but the problem doesn't magically stop on someone's 25th birthday. By the time this book is published, I'll be 25 myself. There's nothing magic about 25 except I can get a rental car myself, and my car insurance may not take as big a bite. Half of all black males are dropping out of high school, and 72 percent of those are unemployed. If you don't work, how do you provide for yourself and your family? By the time they're in their 30s, over 60 percent of these black, male dropouts will have spent at least some time behind bars.

The sad truth is most of these lost young men and women have some stupid media image of making it big—but they have no plan.

> I'm not comfortable being preachy, but more people need to start spending as much time in the library as they do on the basketball court. If they took the idea that they could escape poverty through education, I think it would make a more basic and long-lasting change in the way things happen. What we need are positive, realistic goals and the willingness to work. Hard work and practical goals.
>
> —*Kareem Abdul-Jabbar (Ferdinand Lewis Alcindor Jr.)*

Some people won't like this, but again, the figures speak for themselves. And it's not just African Americans—Hispanics, Caucasians, Asian—every group has tens of thousands of young men and women dropping through the cracks. It's just that African American males in my age group are the most at-risk.

As if the incarceration and dropout figures aren't enough, urban violence is killing African Americans at rates six times that of white Americans, and my age group, from 15 to 24, are in the most danger. In this age group, 85 out of every 100,000 will be killed. Doesn't sound like a lot? The national average is 6 per 100,000. And black boys and men are the main victims. In fact, they are the country's primary victims of violent crime. The blame can be placed on street gangs, crack cocaine, and easy access to handguns. But the core issue, the one at the heart of all this, for all races, always comes back to single-parent homes and their ability to cope with pressures and issues that trap kids into these lousy and deadly lifestyles.

Something's very wrong. I believe the cure starts in the home, and with having supportive, committed parents. Nothing could be more important to build a foundation for a child and, frankly, until you are satisfied you have that kind of relationship, don't have children. If you don't have a solid relationship with your partner, bringing a child into that environment has nothing to do with love for the child or each other. It's a selfish act that hurts each of you, including your child.

Today, half the homes in America are broken by divorce. Following that line, I know a lot of the people reading this book, especially the children, teenagers, and college students, will not have had a consistent, loving two-parent household as an experience growing up, so what I said up at the beginning of this chapter is important: Start where you are right now, with whatever skills or knowledge you have, and determine yourself to do whatever it takes to succeed.

> It isn't where you came from; it's where you're going that counts.
>
> —*Ella Fitzgerald*

Going to school, staying away from drugs and alcohol (and gambling!), and not marrying until you're in your twenties gives you advantages that can't be ignored. Kids who come from broken homes often don't often get the extra help and attention and encouragement that MeShelle's mom gave her. She's an exception, and a big one. Her mom struggled to give MeShelle opportunities her friends in the hood never had, and it almost cost her everything. You may be an exception, too, but even as exceptional as MeShelle's situation was, she had more negatives to overcome than I did.

My dad came out of a broken home also. His father died when he was just a kid and some of the problems that the family had as a result were devastating. Without a strong father figure to guide him, my father went down some rough paths and tripped over a bunch of stumbling blocks. It took him years longer to get up to speed, but one day he consciously decided, "You know what? I'm not going to keep on living like this! *I want better in my life, and for my family.*" He went back to school, and got his degree as an engineer. There was all this greatness bottled up inside him, and it was a double struggle for him to find it, trust it, and develop it. That's what you have to overcome if your home was shattered when you were growing up.

It's amazing how our decisions can affect generations to come. I can't ever remember my brothers or me ever wanting to be basketball players or Hip Hop artists or anything else like that—not firefighters or police officers, either. We all wanted to be engineers like Dad. While I'm not an engineer, my point is that my parents gave me a certain frame of reference, a perception of life, that caused me to set my sights high from an early age. My parents made it clear that anything I wanted in my life was achievable. They did this repeatedly, especially when I tried to get by with normal kid excuses. My parents were my first mentors, and they showed me a way that made me believe. Made me hope.

A single-parent home is an incredibly difficult thing to manage, much more to overcome if you were raised in one. Yeah, that is pretty blunt, but I'm really not attacking you or your family. I'm also not going to join the popular crowd that ignores these issues and loves to give out some kind of welfare "Excuse Checks" to justify failure. It's important to be honest with ourselves, and then take the necessary steps to overcome whatever obstacles we face. *If we don't do it ourselves, no one else will do it for us.*

Get Off of Yourself

Whatever it is that gets your hackles up, get it off your chest and off your shoulder. If talking about your family and home and things like that irritate you and make you feel defensive, **get over it.** I've already told you, I'm not dissing your home, your momma, or your family. This isn't about how good they are, how hard they tried, or whether someone's better than you. All families face trials and tribulations, but single-parent homes have it the hardest. And the children raised in single-parent homes suffer the most in school and in life.

If this is your life and you feel sorry for yourself, I can't blame you too much. But get over it already! You have a right to be upset about the cards you have been dealt. But if you never ever get beyond being depressed about your crappy life, you'll never get anywhere, will you? So let's start getting over it, okay?

Nobody sets out and says, "I want to raise my own kid with no help and no insurance, work three jobs, never have time for my own life, play the odds that my child will probably dropout and have a dead-end, low-paying job his whole life, or do drugs or go to jail, and practically guarantee he'll have everything else tough in his life, too." Nope, what happens is that boys and girls hear the rappers and watch the videos on BET and MTV, they see the ads and read the *Cosmo* and *Ebony* and *Jet* articles and watch the movies. They see the bling and hear the bang. To them, the good life looks like one big party.

The girls start wanting a baby like it's a status symbol, and the boys start wanting another notch in their belt of "manhood." That's the bottom line. Love, American style. Before anyone thinks any further than their own hormones, a baby pops out and another life is pulled into this mess. No, nobody ever starts out to create a difficult life on purpose, and to cause their children to suffer. But many do, anyway.

A lot of people are going to say, "Well, I didn't have a two-parent household, and I didn't have the advantages you had. So what am I, shut out?"

Of course not! You may have added disadvantages to overcome, but there are hundreds of thousands of successful people who have overcome those same disadvantages in their lives. What I'm really saying here is, if you don't have a two-parent household, or if you're not happy with the role model that your parents are providing you, **get a replacement,** and get on with your life!

I think one of the most important things I learned from my family was the value of **mentorship.** When you're young, and adults spend time with you, you model yourself after them. Later, when we want to grow in a career, we may find a mentor to guide us. An adult male may not be your real father but he may become a father figure, someone you look up to . . . the same is true for mother figures. You can learn things about life from these people, from their experience. In a lot of ways, a mentor can take the place of the parent you don't have. They exist out there but you have to find them. If you didn't like the car you had, you'd get another one, right? So get focused and work toward finding yourself a mentor.

There are so many really good mentors out there, just waiting to help you, to guide you, to be a good role model. Mentors are on sale right now and you know how much they cost? They're free. All these baby boomers coming into retirement have experiences and knowledge that's sitting around, not being used anymore. The easiest time to get a mentor is when you are in school. Just grab a mentor and take responsibility for getting what you need to succeed in life.

We'll spend a whole chapter talking about mentors and how to choose them because they're the most important people in your life, whether you know it or not. Mentors are the people who will help you shortcut the system and learn to work smarter, not harder. So you can reach your goals—and have your treasure—while you're still young enough to really enjoy it.

Right now, let's look at more at the mindset you as their Mentee, their apprentice if you prefer, need to succeed.

> There are no secrets to success: Don't waste time looking for them. Success is the result of perfection, hard work, learning from failure, loyalty to those for whom you work, and persistence.
>
> —*Colin Powell*

Hey, if it was easy, everyone would be successful. Instead, only about 1 or 2 out of every 100 entrepreneurs make it. The rest fail. The rest won't pay the price and take the time to do it right.

Instant gratification doesn't exist. Anything worth having is worth working for—right now. The real question is, do you want to slave away for a worker's wage your whole life? Do you want to continue to work until you're old and broken and using a walker to get around? Do you really want to go on vacations when you're too old to know that you look like a dork because you're so out of touch you think black calf socks and Bermuda shorts is some kind of style statement? Not me!

Look, nobody wants to work, but unless you were born with money, you don't have a choice. Not working for our "daily bread" is not an option. That's the curse Adam chose when he figured he'd found an easier way to get the knowledge of his mentor, God. You *are* going to work, and work hard, but hopefully along the way you'll learn to work smart as well. You really don't have to reinvent the wheel, all you have to do is put some rims and tires on it so it drives smoother, runs easier, and then improve on it—but don't go out and spend years recreating the same thing, or get too caught up in buying spinners and trying to look all rich and successful. Take advantage of the knowledge of people who've gone ahead of you to shorten your growth curve, and get yourself and your dream up and running first.

You Can Work Harder, or You Can Work Smarter

I believe the hardest work is work you have to do for someone else. There's just something mentally grinding about it. While we should all be grateful for the opportunity to earn money and support our family, it's hard to get into the mindset that we're doing it for ourselves, when in reality we're doing the work for someone else and their approval. Working smart really means thinking about the path we're on and deciding if it's the path that really suits us—not necessarily the easiest path, and not necessarily the most comfortable, but the one that gets us to our goal the fastest. As you think about this, picture two roads through life. I call them "Option One" and "Option Two."

Option One: Work 40 to 50 Years for Somebody Else

Do as little as possible to keep the boss happy, after all, the one who pays you is buying your time. You're not giving it away, you're selling it: the one buying your time is *buying* the hours of your life. That's why it's called being a wage-slave. You've sold out to the highest bidder . . . maybe not even the highest. Along the way, you trade one owner for another. Sometimes they leave you hanging, struggling to find another owner to sell your life to. Hours for dollars. That's all you know. Literally shortening your life, by selling off the hours and the days, the months and the years.

Take a couple weeks each year for a vacation. Show up every day at 8, go home around 6. Paint your house on weekends and try to build a little savings account up so you don't have to eat cat food when you finally retire. IF you retire, that is, and don't have a chest blowout by age 45 or 50. Keep your head down, don't create too many waves, and try not to attract too much attention.

Life's a Beach

It's sort of like walking down the beach, and it's crammed with lots of people like on the Fourth of July. You stop every so often to pick up a shell or two. Those are the new skills, new promotions, and life changes along the way. Your real goal is the treasure at the end of the beach, your retirement—the time when you don't have to work. When you can play all day and party all night. But you can take as long as you want to reach it. Spend a few years in school figuring out what you want to be when you grow up. Chill out for a few more years digging sandcastles if you want. No worries. *Hakuna Matata!* You've got plenty of time. It's your life, after all. Don't worry—be happy! Sometimes the whole deal fakes us out so much we actually feel like we're in control!

The only problem is, at this pace, it takes years and years to reach your goal, and your treasure is washing out to sea more and more with every wave, every minute, every day. How much of your goal, your prize, will be there when you finally make it? Who knows? It's more uncertain now than ever, because retirement programs are being raided, social security is being gutted, gas costs more than $3 a gallon, medical costs are rising, and very few people even start thinking about retirement until it's too late. When you finally get to your goal decades later, you find just a few shekels stuck in the sand where your treasure was supposed to be, and another beach full of people ahead of you. Broken, worn-out, broke people mostly sitting and wondering what went wrong.

For people who choose Option One, life drags by, day after day, paycheck to paycheck, "blue Mondays" to TGIF, weekend to weekend, vacation to vacation, finally retirement . . . then it's gone. Game over. One day you wake up and you're dead.

Next time you go shopping, ask the old dude greeting you at the door. He'll tell you.

Option Two: Make a Decision to Get All the Knowledge You Can and Keep Growing Even While You're Working

This option might read: "Swallow your vegetables and liver fast, so you can sink your teeth into that hot apple pie a la mode."

I think of this option as running down the beach and stooping down to pick up those shells (new knowledge, new skills) without missing a step. You get tired, you stumble, but you get back up and keep running. For how long? Sometimes it may seem like forever, but you know you're closing in on the goal a whole lot faster, and when you get there, there's a whole lot more of it to enjoy. Not only that, but you notice how uncrowded this beach is . . . very few people around, and they're all running in the same direction. Nobody's dragging their heels here, wasting years in the sand. They know there's a prize up ahead. You get there after a few years, and there's this monstrous pile of gold, more than you can spend. Plenty to enjoy, to create a lifestyle and a future for your family, and plenty to share with your church and charities.

Just past the pile of gold is another beach, and there aren't many people on it, either. They're all full of life and enjoying every moment. That's the rest of your life, and you're still young so you'll be able to really enjoy it to the max, too! You've won your race, you've claimed your prize and you own your life. You own your own minutes and hours, and you pay yourself royally. You have your health, your family, your financial security.

Enjoying the Journey

Hey, it sounds pretty great, doesn't it. Think about that goal, of owning your own life and doing what you want. What so many people try to avoid is the running, the work. Because running is working double-hard, working double-smart, doing everything above-and-beyond. One of my mentors put it this way:

*I'm willing to do things other people won't do, to live the life others will
never live.*

How about you? Only you can make that decision. And you
make it every day of your life. With every victory you know deeper
and deeper you have the power inside you to overcome whatever
comes your way. You build confidence, you overcome your fear, you
become a champion. And you truly start taking responsibility for your
own successes and failures . . . your own life.

SECTION II

Taking Responsibility for Your Own Life

You have *nobody* but yourself to blame or credit for your successes or failures in life. You have the ability to overcome anything and everything in your life that's holding you back from your dreams. Period. Your ability is enough to overcome *any* obstacle.

Have you ever had a boss or coworker take credit for your work? Maybe they even got a promotion based on things you had done. How did it feel? Who wants to give other people the control over their lives so that they can claim credit for your successes?

Well, we can't blame anyone else for the things in our lives that we don't like, either. You can't have it both ways. You have 100 percent control over your thoughts, your mind, your emotions, and your determination to succeed. Your success—and your failure—are in your hands alone. Nobody else's.

But You Don't Know What I've Been Through!

You had to drop out of school and work to support your family, and couldn't get your diploma? That was then; this is now. What are you going to do with what you've got, where you're at? Work harder, take night school courses, or whatever else you need. Start there, and move ahead.

Oh, but you suffered poverty, and lived in fear of crime and drug dealers in the inner city? Hey, you're no refugee from some war-torn country! Nobody's hunting you down and killing you, like in Bosnia or Iraq, or Rwanda or Sudan. There's no "line," no "street" you can't cross and take on a new life. People drive, fly, walk thousands of miles, crowd on little bitty boats and inner tubes and go out into the open ocean just to get here, just to make it to America . . . with *nothing!* And they make it . . . and you've got it better than they ever did.

Maybe you were physically or sexually abused as a child, or even as an adult. Some people live with the pain, the shame, and the fear for the rest of their life. Why hold on? Give it up to God and get on with your life.

The Americans with Disabilities Act proved that people with every kind of physical and mental handicap are determined *and able* to overcome these things and live complete lives. Man, they don't even want you to use the word *handicapped* because they don't see themselves as lacking in any way! It's not like they're celebrating their illness or disability, these are just people who've decided, just like my dad and my wife MeShelle, "You know what? I'm not going to let this beat me down! I want better in my life!"

What about those of us who aren't disabled? Is there any rational way we can still make excuses like someone might believe our life really is beyond our control? *You are responsible for your own life!*

How can anyone born in America see the incredible success that homeless, penniless immigrants can achieve, and still hold onto feeble excuses? Give it up!

If someone can come over here, speaking no English, from some country with a caste system or where terrorists could strike at any minute, *with nothing in their pockets* and STILL make something of their lives . . . what's YOUR excuse!? What is so big that it can hold you back in America, with all the advantages we have and everything?

To assume any of the excuses we hear are even remotely real *reasons* why people fail is a lot like saying the slaves should have had plenty of reasons for failing after the Civil War. Duh! Of course they had loads of reasons that were real, crippling historical facts. After all, they'd endured generations of complete control and bondage—physical, sexual, and psychological abuse. They had no voice, no rights, no options except to try to escape. And the penalty for that was death.

Did they use any of these as an excuse for failure in their lives? No! They created a rich culture of song and art and storytelling. They kept the flame of hope alive. Free blacks studied at whatever school they could, tapped into any knowledge resources available, and became leaders and orators against slavery. There were even black colleges and universities founded, like Cheyney University, created in 1837.

In the first 30 years after the Civil War ended, literacy among former slaves skyrocketed from 30 percent to over 70 percent, and thousands of black-owned businesses were started. Before 1900, 75 black colleges were founded. And they kept overcoming through Jim Crow, segregation, unequal pay and working conditions, and schools that got secondhand everything, if they were lucky!

We have no excuses today that hold a candle to what those people went through. I won't even bother ripping apart the "culture of racism" or "systemic racism" excuse. I'm black, so don't even try that one with me! Or I'll start listing off hundreds of incredible people of my race and your race and any other race you want, and show you thousands, no, *hundreds* of thousands who've made it in spite of any and every obstacle placed before them.

Tell the black South African who endured apartheid, or the Nigerian, or the Central American immigrant who finally made it to this country, that racism here is somehow responsible for someone's failure. He won't understand, since his English isn't as good as yours, and he never finished sixth grade. But give him a few years, until he's acquired a few motels or minute markets, or built some other business empire, and try to tell him again. See if you can do it with a straight face. All the excuses in the world don't matter, so drop the excuses and get going with your life.

> My great concern is not whether you have failed, but whether you are content with your failure.
>
> —*Abraham Lincoln*

I'm not discounting how difficult your life may have been for you, or may be right now. No matter what you're going through, someone else has gone through the same or worse, and others are going through situations that are so bad we can't even imagine it. But they have made it, and so can you. As Jesse Jackson said to the 1988 Democratic Convention:

I was born in the slum, but the slum was not born in me. And it wasn't born in you, and you can make it. Hold your head high, stick your chest out. You can make it.

It doesn't really matter what the excuse is: broken homes, drugs, prostitution . . . I've probably met 30 or a hundred or a thousand other people that overcame the same thing, or something even worse.

So, is there really any excuse that somebody can have in the United States for a failed life? It's all in our perception! Any circumstance in your life can be overcome. **If you think you can, or if you think you can't . . . you're right!** And whatever you think, whatever your perception is, will become your reality.

The Black Hole of Excuses

Two of the most powerful things that have given me the successes I've had in my life are not accepting the words: *"You can't do that,"* and not giving myself excuses for failure. My determination has always been to do the things necessary to accomplish my goals and dreams, to make things happen instead of waiting for something to happen.

When I decided to create video games, I stayed focused on doing that and I didn't stop until it happened. When I saw a need for a job search portal for teens, I did what it took, including making financial presentations to adults three and four times my age, and getting their money for my business. When the opportunity came to take on my first big real estate development, I took on tasks I didn't even know were going to be required . . . whatever it took. And in the energy resources field I'm in totally unknown territory, but I have the vision and we'll do whatever is necessary to make it succeed.

But what I have learned along the way is that most people aren't comfortable committing, aren't ready to do, actually do, what needs to be done to really achieve their goals. They like the idea of success but not the commitment and hard work to get it. They never realize their full potential and never seize the opportunities that are right in front of them because they can't stop thinking of all the negative reasons why they can't reach their goals. There's a great, old poem about this that one of my mentors sent me. This says it all:

If You Think You Are Beaten

If you think your are beaten, you are,
If you think that you dare not, you don't,

If you like to win, but think you can't,
It's almost certain you won't.
If you think you'll lose, you've lost,
For out in the world you'll find
Success begins with a fellow's will;
It's all in the state of mind.
If you think you are out-classed, you are;
You've got to think high to rise;
You've got to be sure of yourself before
You can ever win a prize.
Life's battles don't always go
To the stronger or faster man;
But sooner or later the man who wins
Is the man who thinks he can!

—Anonymous

In fact, that pretty much sums up everything we've discussed up until now. Whether we want to believe it, it's the gray matter between our ears that holds us back, not other people or circumstances. It's a choice that we make to overcome fear, and a decision we make to take action on our dreams.

In my entrepreneurism classes, I share with my students ways that they can start their own business like I did, and start making some money even while they're still in school. I have my students give me their ideas for a business. Then I challenge them to throw out all the reasons why an idea wouldn't work. Immediately, the excuses start flying.

One by one I strip away every excuse they come up with. What we end up with is the fact that almost nothing is impossible for a determined person. Let's look at some of the excuses people might throw out to convince themselves, or others, that "It can't be done" or "I can't do it."

"Well, sure, *you* could do that Mr. Taylor, but I sure can't because I'm not smart like you."

"You gotta have some money to get going, and I don't have any money."

"Mr. Taylor, you know all about business and stuff, but I don't, so how could I possibly start a company?"

"I'm a girl, who'd listen to my ideas?"

The excuses go on and on and on, and it's sad to see it happen because I know—*and now you know*—what will happen as a result. These people will never even try. If they're already making excuses for their life in high school, what happens to those students who find themselves a single parent, broke, homeless, and with a child to support?

What Excuse in Your Life Is Worth Forgetting about Your Dreams?

In the movie *The Pursuit of Happyness*, Will Smith plays a real-life homeless father, Chris Gardner, who understood "whatever it takes." Gardner, and his son Christopher, are reduced by the circumstances of life to live on the street, even as he pursued his dream of a better life. He lands an internship with stockbroker giant Dean Witter, but it's not even a paying job for months.

Chris Gardner's real-life experiences exemplify his courage, strength, and his will to overcome any obstacle in the way of his vision of a better life. By day he projects the image of a successful businessman, while his boss and clients remain totally unaware of how desperate his life really is, how close to the edge he's hanging on. After work each day, he races to get a flophouse bed at a church mission, and is sometimes forced to sleep wherever they can find a safe spot . . . at one point, he and his son are even forced to "camp" in the Oakland BART station restroom!

But he didn't give up. He didn't give in. He was determined to find a way through—or over, or under, or around—every fresh obstacle and life circumstance that knocked him down. And he did it all with such an incredible attitude, that he never forgot that he was a father, and so he made the entire ordeal seem like a game that dad and son were playing together, having an adventure.

Gardner did make it, and make it big. He became the top intern, the only one of his class that was finally hired, and he became incredibly successful. Today, he owns his own multimillion-dollar brokerage house. He never let excuses stop him, and neither should you.

If You Think You Can, or If You Think You Can't, You're Right!

When you throw out a bunch of reasons why you *can't* do something, they usually come true. You won't do it. It's like something just happens in your mind and your brain goes to work overtime supporting that line of reasoning. Eventually, you'll convince yourself that all those forces out there in the world are working against you, just as if they held a meeting and "they" decided you are going to fail. Naturally, this is crazy thinking but you'd be surprised how many people talk this way, and think this way, and live out their lives as though this is the way it really is.

Instead of limiting your life with all the "can'ts," why not decide to look at what you *can* do instead? With a simple change of focus, you can look at opportunities instead of problems. Steve Covey, in his book *Seven Habits of Highly Successful People* called it "focusing on the outcome" (New York: Simon & Schuster, 1989).

When You Focus on Your Ultimate Goal, Excuses Stop Being Part of Your Thinking

There's just no place for excuses. All of a sudden, your brain channels all your thoughts into goal-oriented ideas and actions. If you don't have a car to get where you need to go, you take a cab. If you can't afford a cab, you take a bicycle. If you don't have a bicycle, you walk. Need more information? You go to the library. Need money? You take on a second job, even a third. You find venture capital groups and angel investors to talk to. You find investors, partners, family members, or even a bank that will give it to you. You find a way.

How you get there is not the problem, the important thing is getting there!

When my goal was to become the CEO of a publicly traded company, it didn't matter that I had never done it before. It didn't matter that I didn't have the foggiest notion of how to go about making a public stock offering, dealing with the SEC and shareholders, or any of the other things I've experienced today. What *was* important was that

I determined I *would* get it done . . . *somehow*. As a result, going public became my number one focus and before I knew it, there I was, the youngest African American CEO of any public company in history. I didn't stop there. Now my focus is on newer, even bigger goals.

An interesting thing happens when you develop a passion and you focus on a serious goal—you find resources in your brain you never knew you had. Many years ago, there was a young man named Tom who was a very poor student in school. Tom was partially deaf and his mind tended to wander and he daydreamed a lot, so much so his teacher called him "addled," or retarded. After only a few months of school, he was sent home where his mother continued Tom's education.

Apparently, school didn't interest Tom. What he did find interesting was figuring things out, inventing things, solving problems. In fact, he'd get so wrapped up in a project that he would hardly sleep at all. He'd only take short 15 or 20 minute catnaps, and work around the clock.

One particular project got Tom really excited, and he worked on it day and night. He had an idea about something that nobody had ever done before. His goal was clear to him and he was convinced it could be done even though many other people had tried it unsuccessfully. He tried one thing after another and nothing worked. Literally hundreds of possible solutions all failed. Then thousands. How did he keep on in the face of such failure? When asked, he said, **"I am not discouraged, because every wrong attempt discarded is another step forward."**

I haven't failed. I've just found 10,000 ways that won't work.

Finally, after *10,000* failed attempts, he found the right combination to make his idea a success. The result was the world's first electric lightbulb—an invention that made Thomas Alva Edison rich and famous throughout the world and throughout history.

Every time I think about Edison I wonder, "What if he had stopped at 9,999? How much longer before someone else would be willing to keep working toward their dream? How many more years would we have lived in a world of gaslights and candles?"

Focus on What You *Can* Do, Not What You Can't Do

We can get angry and shout and complain about the Man, the boss, the government, whites, blacks, Asians, or Indians taking jobs; Mexicans crossing the border, our ex-wife or husband, our parents, or on and on. Maybe this describes you. If it does, I'm sorry if it hurts your feelings but I'm going to be straight with you. In my opinion, excuses are used by only two types of people: *Those who are just lazy and only care about right now, and those who are too afraid to get up and make something happen.*

If you're lazy, unless you pull yourself up and get serious about your dreams there is no way I can help you attain success. Might as well close this book here. Success in any area of life takes a lot of effort and initiative. Period. You cannot be lazy and have control over your life. You may think you do, but the reality is you've chosen to sell your birthright for a bowl of gruel. You have the ability to achieve, but you've got to get up offa that thang and work it.

> Look to the ant, thou sluggard!
>
> —*Proverbs 6:6*

People who are lazy are in it for the instant gratification. The feel good. The now. They'll even tell you that. "Live for today." Like the grasshopper and the ant: "You're crazy to work so hard. Relax. Let's party! We can worry about tomorrow when it comes." But remember, the grasshopper was starving and freezing in the end, while the ant was warm and had a good place to store food for the winter.

Giving Up Control

Bad things—like the grasshopper starving or freezing—are beyond our control, at least that's the excuse. Usually, when good things happen, people who use excuses and blame will usually credit other outside forces like "Lady Luck." Sadly, they feel—really believe—that they are powerless to make their life any different. Other people and other forces control the direction of their life, and they have basically given up any desire to control their life themselves. They are slaves and don't even know it.

You will find at least one of these people in almost every workplace. Just think of the loudest and bitterest complainer you know, the one who is always bellyaching. They complain about the management, their working conditions, the traffic, the politicians, or the rotten things done to them by others. People like this never seem to run out of things to carp about because there is so much that's unfair in their lives. They have too much work. They're not appreciated. "Oh, poor me!" they cry, "Why me? Why is it always me?"

Get Over It!

I'm not saying there are easy answers to every problem, but at some point you have to stop whining, suck it up, and get going. I know too many people who live life as losers, and not because they don't have talent and ability. In fact, some of them have more ability than people I meet who are already running successful businesses. It's because they let all their excuses keep them boxed in and *they never put their abilities to work*. Instead, they sit and complain to their friends about how great things could have been *if only* this or that thing hadn't kept them back.

> *It is better to have tried something great and failed,*
> *than to have tried nothing at all and succeeded.*

The thing that bothers me most about excuses is that when you get right down to it, 80 percent of all excuses exist only in the person's head. In other words, the obstacle is there because the person has put it there, or has accepted their perception as their reality, regardless of any evidence to the contrary. I'll prove it to you.

Excuse Number One: I Don't Have the Money

It takes money to make money, right? There is no sin or shame in not having a lot of money. The greatest success stories of all started out with humble beginnings. Remember the shack I lived in, without even hot water for our baths? But by now you should realize that using *anything* we lack as an excuse—education, experience, time, money—is a sure way never to achieve our full potential in life.

"No money" is probably the most-used excuse for not pursuing dreams and goals. Essentially, this excuse asks us to believe that we would be able to be more successful if we had access to more capital. The reality is more businesses have probably failed by assuming they could throw money at their problems, instead of dealing with the problems and making hard changes, than have failed from not having enough money. Both are management, not money, issues.

It's really our inflated perception of the risks involved that kills the deal. We fret and worry about the unknown, develop all sorts of expectations that are usually proven false anyway. The risks grow and grow in our minds, and the scales tip further and further away from our dream and back to the safety of our "Comfort Zone." The safety of our mental prison becomes preferable to the danger of the unknown world.

Exactly How Much Money Do You Really Need?

Having "enough" money is about as vague as it gets. How much is enough? Other than your monthly expenses, and three to six months' income for emergencies, any other money is the available capital you can use to grow. That can be equity tied up in your home, credit cards, savings.

A lot of times people can find the extra capital they need just by getting serious about budgeting and cutting their costs. I've known people who lived in a van and ate peanut butter and popcorn for months, just to get to their goal and realize their dream. Going out on weekends, driving too fast and wasting gas, smoking, drinking, buying name brands, paying new car payments, renting expensive apartments, overeating . . . there are scores of ways we waste the pennies and dollars we have. Only you can decide how you can cut your costs. The problem is, most never budget . . . after all, you make it, you should be able to spend it, right? Right! So do you want to waste it on junk, or invest in your dreams?

The $90,000 Cup of Coffee

I have a friend who stops at Starbucks every morning on his way into work. He makes six figures, so four bucks for a cup of coffee is no big deal, right? Besides, he deserves it. He's worth it. He works hard, and it's his little extravagance. Do I need to keep listing his rationale—his *excuses?*—I don't think so.

Let's look at the numbers:

$$5\ (\$4.00) \text{ cups a week} \times 50 \text{ weeks} = \$1,000 \text{ a year} \times 30 \text{ years} \times 6\% = \$89,545.17$$

His choice, to spend four bucks a day on coffee, is really a $90,000 decision . . . and my friend doesn't even know it.

I don't know about you, but it makes me think about all the sodas and bottled water and other things I used to casually buy every day for a few bucks. Let's say he opted for the coffee at his office every day. In some offices, the coffee is free, or everyone takes turns buying a can throughout the year. At his office, it costs a quarter a cup. This one small change would mean my friend could **keep an extra $74,117.05** at his retirement party in 30 years.

This kind of money can be earned from our cups of coffee, or the lunches we buy out, or the packs of cigarettes, or the designer wines we drink. It can be the cute holiday decorations and the great sale items we just have to have. It can be the $1,500 rims, $200 shoes, designer clothes, jewelry, tattoos, you name it.

I used my friend's coffee habit as just one example to demonstrate how even our smallest, most insignificant decisions can mean big bucks lost—or earned—all because of **the Time Value of Money.** Up until now, you've had the luxury of ignorance. I'd rather you know the true value of your financial decisions, so you'll be equipped to make the decisions that are best for you.

The Time Value of Money

The **Time Value of Money** is a mathematical fact, an exact formula that will always tell us the direct cost, the dollar value (loss) of the fears we hold onto, and the excuses we fall back on every day. Yet 99 percent of the people I meet have never even been taught this information. I believe most businesses fail because their owners just don't have a clue about how the minutes and the hours of each and every day are making, or breaking them. And I don't just mean in some philosophical sense, I mean in actual dollars. The **Time Value of Money** is one law we want working for us, not against us.

The **Time Value of Money** is the basis for compounding interest. Remember my example to my class? Did you stop and figure out how much money they had actually sacked away? **$72,000.** That's right. Saving $150 a month is only $72,000 after 40 years, but *compounding it* changes it to almost a million dollars. Do you think understanding how all this works could be valuable to you in your life?

We would all rather have money in our hand, right now, than at some point down the road. I mean, if your best friend asks to borrow $10 and promises to pay you back Friday, do you want Friday to come and have her ask you to give her a few more weeks? No! You want it now, not a month from now. We seem to know there's more value in having it today, but is there really any difference in what the money itself is actually worth today versus tomorrow? Mathematically, there's a big difference.

Let's say you know how you can earn 15 percent a year on your money. Now, answer this question:

Would you rather have someone give you:

A. $5,000 today?

B. $10,000 in 5 years?

C. $20,000 in 10 years?

D. $80,000 in 20 years?

Amazingly, all of the answers are actually all the same exact amount (okay, I rounded them all off to the nearest thousand bucks). Here's what I mean: *Each of these are* **worth** *exactly the same amount of money, just at different points in time.*

B, C, and D are how much today's $5,000 investment would be worth, based on 15 percent interest compounded annually (the reason I used 15 percent as our example is because at 15 percent your money essentially doubles every 5 years, give or take, so it makes the math easier than say, 12 percent or 17 percent). So if you had $5,000 today and invested it earning 15 percent interest a year, it actually would be worth $10,056.79 in 5 years and $81,833 after 20 years. (By the way, if it were compounded monthly it would yield $98,577 at the end.)

If money grows from a small amount to a bigger amount in the future, then a bigger, future amount would also be worth a lower dollar amount today, right? So that $20,000 you *could* have 10 years from now is worth only $5,000 today (still figuring you're able to earn 15 percent). The math works both ways.

The real question is, if someone just gave you $5,000, or if you saved that much to invest, would *you* really be able to turn it into *more* than $40,000 over the next 15 years?

Sure you could. You would need to be invested in something that brought you more than 15 percent return on investment (ROI), and they are available. We've had clients who earned more than that in a month or two, so there are many ways to earn double-digit returns.

Have I Lost You?

If you feel a little lost, don't worry. They don't teach you this in most public schools. This is too important for you to miss, and getting hold of it now will change the way you look at money forever. Go ahead and read this section through anyway. Then read it from the beginning again until you start to understand how it all works.

The Time Value of Money is a law, a mathematical
certainty that is the force behind every return on
every investment ever made.

There are different mathematical formulas that show how it works. The example here uses what's called the *Rule of 72*:

If you divide 72 by the interest rate you think you can receive, the
answer will tell you how many years it will take to double your
money.

Doubling your money is a good benchmark for the return you get on any investment. Whether you were to buy a house, or a business, or put your money into a bank account, this rule will work for you.

Let's say I can get 6 percent a year. 72 ÷ 9 = Whew! 12 years. Divide 72 by 10 and you get 7.2 years. I like using the 15 percent return as a rule of thumb, because doubling my money every 5 years makes for easy math. But what if you were able to make 30 percent, 40 percent, or more? It's possible in real estate and other investments.

What if you could make 100 percent ROI in a year? It's possible, and I've done it. It's also possible by investing and reinvesting your profits several times in the same year. Even if you've never looked at the possibility of buying a home for yourself or as an investment, you can see the math pretty easy this way, and real estate is all around us, so it's more familiar than say, stocks and bonds. For this example let's figure we're buying with cash right now to make it even easier to see how it all works:

You start with $100,000 and buy a house.
You sell it for $133,000 after four months. You made $33,000.

You manage to do this three times over a year, and you've basically made 100 percent on your original investment:

$$33,000 \times 3 = \$99,000 + \text{your original } \$100,000 = \$199,000$$

One of the great things about real estate is that it's pretty easy to leverage your money with real estate, so you can invest using only a little cash, or none at all. What if you were leveraging these purchases completely, using no money down?

> *Remember: The Time Value of Money is a law, a mathematical fact, as absolute as $E = mc^2$ or any other universal mathematical laws. And it will work for us—or against us.*

Every decision or indecision, every positive action or delayed action, gets magnified and multiplied many times over by the compounding interest we gain or lose. Every delay potentially costs us tens of thousands of dollars. Every positive decision potentially *earns us* tens of thousands as well. Every dollar spent, or saved, matters. There are no exceptions—every monetary decision, every one, *every one*.

Not being willing to address financial problems early on can lead to all sorts of problems down the road. Easy credit without credit or financial education is drowning our country in debt. More marriages fail because of a lack of understanding finances, an inability to even talk about financial plans and budgets, or just a plain lack of discipline when it comes to money. Credit is not free money, and it should be treated just like money: if you can't afford to pay off those cards at the end of the month, don't buy.

Budgeting

Create a budget in your personal life now, so you can be disciplined enough to run a business on a budget later.

If you're having trouble making ends meet right now, there are only two possible solutions: either cut your spending or increase your income. As hard as it may seem, budgeting to cut spending is the easier of the two choices. Making more money may mean taking on two, even three jobs so you can save up enough to pay off your debts and get going. Most likely, you can get to your goals a lot sooner once you cut the fat out of your budget. I've found most companies that start on a shoestring learn early how to make the most out of every dollar . . . and they keep getting more bang for their buck even after they're successful.

Credit May Be the Answer

While we're talking about money and equity, let's talk about using credit to fund your dream. Your good credit is a powerful investment tool that can be used without any cash, but has the power to create tens of thousands of dollars of new investment capital—money in your pocket—every year.

I know right now some of you are saying, "I wish someone had told me this before I skated on my cable bill, got behind on my car payments, and defaulted on my student loans."

Take Charge of Your Credit

Many people have never thought of their credit this way. In fact, most people only think of credit when they want to buy something, like a car, or gas, or furniture, or go on a hot date. Credit is a convenience, and it lets us leverage our money in a lot of ways. What do we do when we need a car? We finance it. So we leverage ourselves with a small amount of money down, and finance a large amount of money so we can get a car. Only too often we mix up leveraging our money with living beyond our means.

Living beyond our means is buying too much car, or dropping our credit cards every time we hit an impulse sale, or deciding we want that flat screen plasma television, even though we don't have the cash to pay for it. We do this enough and we get buried in debt, paying minimum payments every single month, running out of money before we run out of month.

Being overextended on credit is no fun. If any of these describe you, the first thing you need to do regarding your credit is to stop the bleeding. Are you:

- Always running out of cash, having to hit the ATM?
- Paying only the minimum payments every month?
- Sending late payments on important things like your rent or mortgage?
- Finding it's taking you a lot longer than you'd figured it would take to pay off balances on your credit cards, finance company bills, and so on?
- Using one account to pay another one? This is a real dangerous financial pyramid that will bring you down fast.

The average credit card balance is $1,700, and less than a third of credit card holders pay off their cards in full each month. Most only pay the minimum payments (American Bankers Association data). This all adds up. Some end up in big trouble.

In just the fist half of 2006, a record 1.3 million Americans filed for bankruptcy according to data from the Administrative Office of the U.S. Courts.

Let's say you pay the minimum of $50 each month on your maxed out $3,000 credit card at 18.9 percent interest. Most people ignore that rate, and just use their plastic like it's Monopoly money. You know how long it'll take you to pay off that card (assuming you cut it up and never use it again)? Over 15 years. Oh, and the interest charges will be more than *triple* your balance. ***You'll pay over $6,200 in interest ALONE.***

Just adding $10 more to your payment will cut it down to about 8 years to pay it off, and you'll save over half the interest. (You'll still pay almost $3,000 in interest on top of your $3,000 balance.) We'll talk more about how this works later.

Taking Control of Your Bills, Your Spending, and Your Credit Is Vital

When you have good credit, it can be used for good investments, not just spending on junk. Investing by using your credit cannot only cover your interest payments, it can create a pool of money that can grow, and grow, and grow, with your money working for you (instead of you always having to work for more money). But what exactly *is* good credit and who determines whether we qualify?

Do you really know what's been reported in your credit record up until now? Most people I talk with have a passive attitude toward their credit. We tend to assume that credit reporting is somehow an automatic process. They try to pay their bills on time, and most have never contacted a Credit Bureau directly, or know what's in their credit report.

I suggest you at least check your credit once a year, just because it's free and you should know what's being reported on you. I subscribe to an online service that notifies me if any inquiry or change takes place in my credit file, or if anyone tries to use my credit or identity. Identity theft is becoming more and more of a problem, and that alone is a good enough reason to pay $50 a year or so to monitor your credit.

Which bureau should you use to check your credit? Here are the three biggies:

1. *Equifax:* www.equifax.com or 800-685-1111
2. *Experian:* www.experian.com or 800-682-7654
3. *TransUnion:* www.transunion.com or 800-916-8800

After you download your report, read the explanations for the codes used and check it to see if there are any errors. You're going to want to dispute these with the individual bureaus before you go and apply with a bank or lender for a loan, and they pull the information.

Other things to check (and dispute if they're wrong) include:

- Personal information like your address, birthday, social security number, and your employment record.
- Make sure all the credit accounts they are showing are yours, and that the information is right. You may also find some accounts with bad information or worse, accounts that you don't even recognize as yours. Sometimes a good account may be there, but might not have been reported properly.
- How many 30-day, 60-day, or 90-day late payments show? A lot of people don't see what the fuss is about when something is "30-days" late. It means you paid *60 days* after your statement date. If someone owed you money and took two months to get their payment to you, do you think you'd get a little hot? Banks and creditors expect you to pay *by* your due date, period.
- What are the highest reported credit lines? How do they report your payment history? Make sure if you borrowed $10,000 for a car three years ago and paid it off, that it shows the high credit and that the balance is zero. Rotating credit cards should show the high balance and the current balance on the card. If you pay it off every month, that should be zero, too.
- Any legal notices, liens, or judgments? A lot of time people are surprised when they find liens from apartments or from the cable company, or from a doctor or whoever. They may not even realize they have a $36 outstanding bill from some apartment where they lived five years ago, and that the apartment made it public record. Best to try to settle it and get it taken off your report.
- Have you been through bankruptcy? If so, does it show as being discharged?

Anything that's wrong on your report needs to be dealt with right away, with whatever bureaus show the mistakes. The law requires credit-reporting agencies to deal with any dispute within a "reasonable period of time." This generally means 30 days. You can contact them by phone, but sometimes they require you to file your dispute in writing, sometimes online. Expect them to ask for supporting documents.

Every little thing, taken together, creates the overall picture of your creditworthiness. For example, lenders even look at little things like how many inquiries you've had over the past six months; but relax, your personal inquiries don't count since it's for personal information, not a specific credit application.

It's up to you to stay on top of what's being shown in your credit report, and to maintain good, strong credit, because these reports, and the credit rating that comes from them, are all the lenders will see.

Establishing good credit is an ongoing process. You're literally creating a *history* of how well you honor your business and financial obligations. Assuming you continue to be *financially able*, lenders assume if you've acted a certain way up until now, you'll probably continue to act the same with your future credit, too. Lenders sometimes refer to these concepts as the "Four Cs" of credit.

The Four Cs of Credit

There are four main considerations that make the whole credit thing work. As you read over them, you'll realize right away they are pretty **subjective** measurements. Like in business, you present yourself—hopefully—in the best way possible to get the lender to accept that you fulfill all of these points. For most major loans today, lenders use a computer scoring system we'll talk about as well. Regardless, these are the main factors *all* lenders are looking at when they are deciding whether you're a good risk for them. Here are the four Cs:

1. *Character: Will you repay the loan?* This is really what it's all about, isn't it? How have you handled paying your debts up until now? Do you pay bills on time, or cross the line into late payments pretty often? How do you honor your obligations? They're looking at your integrity here.

2. *Capacity: Can you repay the loan?* Do you have enough income to pay? Do you have a steady job, and have you been there awhile? What other sources of income do you have? What's your debt ratio: how much of your take-home pay goes to pay your debts now, and how will this loan change that?

3. *Collateral; What secures the loan?* What's your "Plan B" if you can't pay the loan? Collateral insures that the loan will be repaid,

even if you default, so it's a fail-safe for the lender. On a home loan, the house (and land) is the collateral or security for the debt. On a business loan, it's a little different. You may not have any assets or any collateral to put up to secure the loan. On a business loan, especially starting out, you may find you need to secure it with equity in your company. This would be a percentage of ownership, or a certain amount of stock. Once you pay off the loan, this security can be returned to you, or in some cases used to cover the interest on the loan.

4. *Capital (accumulation): How much are you worth?* How much will this new loan affect your life? Will it really squeeze you? Are you already living paycheck to paycheck? Could one major event wipe out your income, like an accident, divorce, or death? What other assets could you use to repay the debt (savings accounts, certificates of deposit, etc.)?

Ultimately, lenders set their own standards that determine whether or not to give you credit. While business or commercial loans have some of their own standards, most consumer loans are under federal and state Equal Opportunity and Truth in Lending regulations that govern *how* lenders can determine whether to loan you money. To help them rate the more subjective four C's, they may also pull a special credit report that gives them your *credit score*, which is based on all of these factors and more.

Most lenders today use this more objective rating credit scoring system.

What's a Credit Score?

Credit scoring rates you against other consumers with similar profiles, just like standardized tests in the school system. In most scoring systems, you are weighed and graded on five areas:

1. Payment history—35 percent
2. Outstanding credit—30 percent
3. Length of credit history—15 percent
4. New credit loads—10 percent
5. Mix of different types of credit—10 percent

What Is a "Good" Credit Score?

It's not all that important to know your precise score because it changes as your circumstances change, as you pay off loans and take on new ones, as you change jobs and income, and so on. It is, however, a good idea to know what range you're in. Here are examples of the ranges used by most lenders, but bear in mind some companies have different guidelines that may allow for lower or higher credit ranges.

> *750 and up—AAA:* These are the best possible numbers for anyone, and these folks get the lowest interest rates and the best terms. In this range, lenders often need only a little documentation, if any at all. Ever hear of "signature loans?"
>
> *725 to 749—AA:* These are still so high that very little documentation is usually required. Interest rates may be a little higher than AAA, terms on the loans probably about the same.
>
> *680 to 724—A:* Standard conforming rates, standard documentation are required (things like pay stubs, income tax returns, bank account statements, etc.). Still solid gold.
>
> *620 to 679—A–:* Still good credit, but interest rates may be a little higher and full documentation is required.
>
> *580 to 619—B to C:* More limitations, higher rates, more documentation, and more down payment is required.
>
> *500 to 579—D:* Very limited financing options and higher interest will apply.
>
> Below 500—F: Generally, no programs for home mortgages except those requiring significant down payment, like 20 percent to 30 percent or more, and significantly higher interest rates.

Be Prepared

I included all of this information on credit to help you better understand how lenders look at your application when you apply for a loan. The real message is: You need to be *proactive* with your credit. You need to stay on top of your monthly payments and your credit file. And you need to get your debts paid down so you can tap your credit to help you build your dreams.

Your Credit Can Be the Key to Your Future

Can you see how powerful good credit can be? All the credit card companies and retail stores want you to use your credit to buy all the junk out there, but it's worth a lot more than that if you use it wisely. It really can be "money in the bank" today and in the future.

> Earlier, I suggested that your own good credit may be a sleeping giant you never considered in your investing plans. City Capital actually created one program that let regular people with good credit become real estate investors, using none of their cash, *only* their credit. It was a simple concept, but one that took off nationwide. Our successful Credit-Investor program (www.nomoneyinvestment.com) was a very attractive component of our real estate division when we sold our developments in 2007 to allow us to focus more on renewable energy initiatives.

Start with Nothing? Why Not?

I can't tell you the number of successful businesses I know of that started out with a few hundred dollars and some credit cards. Credit lets you leverage more for your business. The key is to work at paying off the balance every month possible to renew the available credit capital for more expansion—more products, more marketing, more staff. Are you beginning to see how powerful credit can be in your life?

What if you can't get any money together at all? First of all, I'd be worried about your entrepreneurial ability if that was the case, but let's leave that aside for now. Is your dream important enough with you to make it happen anyway?

What if all you could pull together to get started was a single paper clip? Do you think you could use that paper clip to start a business? Build your dreams? Get your own home? I can already imagine you snickering, but before you dismiss this idea as pure hogwash, let me tell you a true story, one that was reported widely by the national news media.

An inventive and adventurous young man named Kyle McDonald did what I just described. His plan was to start with a red paperclip and keep trading up until he was able to trade for a house. Crazy idea, isn't it? But Kyle went online and did just that. It took him about a year of trading, but he ended up with a home of his very own . . . all for the starting price of a single paper clip! You can Google Kyle McDonald and read the story for yourself. So what was it you said was stopping you?

Online Opportunities

Since I started in computers and programming, naturally the first place I think of to make some money is the online world. If you have a computer, and the majority of homes in the United States now have at least one, think about how many other businesses can be operated with just a computer. You can get a very good state-of-the-art computer for $300 or $400. Can't afford that? Use the computers at your local library or school . . . they're free. That's what I had to do when I first started out.

Once you have that computer and you're connected to the Internet, you can start any number of online businesses that cost practically zero. You don't need a store, you don't need to print business cards or hang a sign outside the door. You don't need a car, you don't even need to get dressed if you don't want to.

Lots of people want to sell goods on eBay but they don't know how (and don't want to take the time to learn) or they don't have the time. Ever seen a consignment shop, you know, where people take old clothes and things, and the store sells them and keeps part of the profits? With just limited experience, you can easily start a service where you take other peoples' goods on consignment, sell them online, and keep a portion of the profits. Think how simple this is:

- Your customer gives you their product; you don't pay a thing.
- Your customer pays the listing fees and shipping costs out of his or her pocket, so you have no costs.
- You go online and list the products using your own skills.
- When it sells, you make a clear profit in real dollars.

What Does This Do to the "Lack of Capital" Excuse?

You could run something like this in your spare time and still have enough time to do something else (like a job). A couple of days each week a friend of mine goes to stereo shops and electronics repair stores after he leaves his day job. He asks them if they have any abandoned or discontinued stereos or televisions that they would like to get rid of. They always do. He doesn't even have to put the items in his car and take them home. All he needs is a photo and a description. Then he puts these pieces up for sale on eBay.

With some of the store owners, he keeps from $40 to $50 on each sale and they even take care of the listing and shipping costs. With others, they're just happy to have the "junk" out of their shop, and not have to pay to have it hauled away. On those sales, he gets all the profit. My friend loves this business because he can make $1,000 to $2,000 a month with barely any expenses whatsoever. He's saving up his money so he can afford to leave his job and go out on his own.

Maybe you like collectibles or antiques, or going to garage sales. I have a friend who likes Starbucks mugs and antiques. He's pulling over $20,000 in sales off eBay—every month. Almost any area of knowledge or interest will provide everything you need to sell, and sell big online.

There are many other online business opportunities, too. We hire independent contractors all the time who work from home on their computer. A smart person can write newsletters, design logos, layout brochures, type term papers for students, create resumes for job applicants, even write advertising and marketing copy—all without leaving home. In fact, that's how I met Emerson, because I needed marketing and sales help and copywriting. Like him, you may be able to use your existing knowledge and skill to consult with other people.

Offline Opportunities

Before computers, people did childcare, hair styling, alterations, and other businesses, all from their home. Oseola McCarty was a woman whose customers brought their laundry to her house for washing and ironing. A few years ago the national news surprised themselves with all the coverage of this humble washwoman, who gave—before her death—$150,000 of her life's savings to provide scholarships for minority students. She never went to school; she just washed and ironed clothes for a few dollars a bundle. Yet, she became the University of Southern Mississippi's most famous benefactor and helped change the lives of students she never even met.

I'll talk a little more about her later. A lot of people reading this may diss the idea of washing clothes as beneath them, but she didn't let stuff hold her back like other people might. She made a way where others saw no way and changed the lives of people for years down the road.

Real Estate

Even though we've largely moved beyond real estate into biofuels, I still like working in real estate. There's something secure about having tangible, "real" property that you hold title on.

Plus, there's probably no business in the country with more information available on how to sell and buy than real estate investing. You'll find a whole section of books at the bookstore, even more at the library. So access to information isn't an excuse.

In a typical home loan, you, the buyer, may put down say, 10 percent on a $100,000 house. But you get ownership of the entire house, or 10 times your down payment money! You can live in it, rent it, sell it, or just sit on it as an investment. Your choice.

No Money Down

You can even learn to do this so well that you don't have to put down *anything*. Not one penny. I've already mentioned how our company, City Capital, developed a program where investors could own their own investment property with no money down, using only their good credit.

This principle is the same whether it's a house or another company that you're buying. Keep your eye on the prize. **Just do it!**

However you go about it, using real estate can fund your dream. Just lock up a deal on a house, match it with your buyer, go to the closing, and collect a check. With the money you made from the sale, you now have start-up capital. End of story.

I know people who do 5 or 10 houses a year, or even in a month. Some make six figures . . . on one house. Most do it without a partner or lender, sometimes in a simultaneous closing, with their buyer bringing the cash to finalize the deal. Or they option the house and don't need to actually buy it at all to get their payday.

Sure, it takes some time invested to learn this business, but so what? What have you got going that will potentially make you tens of thousands of dollars this fast? Why not hit the library or bookstore and crack open the books and just do it? Anyway, this example should demonstrate once and for all that you don't always need to have money to get started in business. And if you do need money for your business venture, there are plenty of ways to get it.

Are the Obstacles You See Real or Imagined?

I believe any circumstance that someone could use to blame lack of capital as their excuse for failure, is really nothing more than their own perception. When you have a serious desire to achieve something, you can often find ways to locate and free up the hidden and tied-up capital in your life. And when you demonstrate the discipline to manage whatever available money and credit you already have, and have passion and focus on your dream, *nothing* will get in your way! There are angel investors, venture capitalists, and other kinds of investors who will buy into your dream and help you make it a reality. How do I know this?

As a teenager, I was able to convey this passion to rooms full of people who had big money, and they put their money on the table to make my dreams a reality. I personally raised over $250,000 in financing when I was only 17. That money allowed me to grow my company into the highly successful GoFerretGo.com, eventually valued at several million dollars. Follow your dreams and the money will follow you.

More Money than Deals

Something Emerson Brantley told me in our first meeting shocked even me. Emerson also brokers business funding for companies. He said, "Ephren, there's more funding out there and more funds sitting around waiting to be put into valid companies, than there are valid deals." The reason? So many companies sell themselves short, or give up the search empty-handed. Don't ever quit trying until you reach your goal.

For anyone else who's actually tried to get bankers and friends and associates to buy into a dream, this may sound like a joke. But he's right. Deals come to those who are looking for deals. Money comes to those who are looking for money. Notice I said looking, not *wishing*. I mean going out there personally pressing flesh, knocking on doors, making presentations, and asking for it.

Remember: Finding the money and doing something with it are two different things. Application is always the bridge that takes us from where we're at, with whatever knowledge and capital and whatever else we have in our hands, to true success. Application of information and education, maximizing the use of your spare time, using your money wisely, the willingness to make decisions and act. If you need money, get it. If you have some money, use it. And get going. Time's a wasting!

Excuse Number Two: I Don't Have the Time

After lack of capital, lack of time is probably the most-often heard excuse for not doing the things that need to be done in our lives. Feeling too crunched for time to take on anything new. Of not having enough time. Or rather, the *perception* of not having the time: Not having time to get the house painted, no time to exercise, not taking our spouse on dates, not starting our own business, and on and on.

It's also a major excuse that holds individuals and families back from ever realizing their full potential and keeps us from our dreams. The reality is that the busiest people often are the ones who can get the most done with the time they have. And they have exactly the same amount of time as you and I:

> *We all have 24 hours in every day; 168 hours each week; 52 weeks in a year; 525,600 minutes every year.*

I don't get one minute more than you. We all have the exact same number of hours in each day—no more, no less. It's how we manage our minutes and hours that counts. Just like managing our money, managing our time frees us up. Overextending our commitments on our calendars, and wasting "free time" in low-quality ways, buries us emotionally and keeps us too tied up and wiped out to pursue our dreams.

No matter how you look at the finite amount of time we all receive, it is our own responsibility to maximize every second of every minute of every day of our lives. But managing time takes discipline. So perhaps it is the lack of discipline that is the real problem, or the bottom line of all excuses. So, learn to avoid wasting time and to maximize your productive time. But whatever you do, manage some time to pursue your dreams or they'll slip away. You will wake up one day and find that 10, 20, 30, or more years have passed . . . and so have your dreams.

Don't let the excuse of time keep you from achieving the things you want to achieve. To say we never seem to have enough time is really a management and responsibility issue. If we let it keep us away from our dreams, it becomes a deadly excuse.

As we've discussed, we largely create our own reality, in both our personal and business lives. If we perceive the world as our oyster, it becomes that. If we perceive it as a stacked deck against us, chances are our life will reflect this. How often have you witnessed someone literally shooting themselves in the foot, missing the boat when a crystal clear opportunity presented itself? It's true, if we think we can, or if we think we can't, we're right—either way.

Time can be our enemy or our ally, depending on how we perceive it *and* how we act on those perceptions. And there is a *price to action; a cost factor attached to every decision we make*—a cost in our own life—for all of the perceptions and fears we let run our life. People who never have time to adequately focus on their investments, who use time as an excuse to hold themselves back, soon find their reality is a string of disappointing returns on those investments.

Time Is Money; Money Is Time

True enough, time is money. We've all heard this before. But tell this to the single mom with three kids and two jobs. Or the corporate executive who regularly misses his daughter's soccer games because senior management has him overseeing six committees. Remind the middle-aged kindergarten teacher who spends hours each night cutting out craft items for her students because no funding is available for her classroom. Tell it to the hourly worker who makes a good living, but only because he pulls every overtime shift available. I could go on and on . . .

There Really Is a Time Crunch

Two-income households and six-figure mortgages, car repairs, team sports, and the constant American Dream of getting *more* all add up to overworked, underpaid, overstressed, and hopelessly stretched out families. There really are more demands than ever for the minutes of our lives.

Is your life so crunched that you've decided you'll never realize your dreams? Or have you just given in and decided that your dreams have to wait, to go on the back burner until . . .? The minutes we have *now* are all we can be sure of. Using what we have *now* is what matters.

> *It's not about how* much *time we have. It's about how we use the minutes of our lives every day.*

We are time crunched today because of decisions we ourselves have made, like where we live affects the jobs we hold and how long our commute time is. I know people who drive or ride three to four hours roundtrip a day, every day. Does that pinch their available time? You bet it does.

We choose the activities and the priorities in our lives. Going to church once or twice a week takes a few hours. But so does watching all the Sunday afternoon ball games, or deciding to spend hours working on our plumbing to save the cost of a plumber (number one rule for real estate investors: use a contractor, don't do it yourself). Taking an hour and a half to get ourselves together in the mornings, listening to endless voice mail messages, joining the softball team at work, and running our kids around to every conceivable activity and sport . . . everything we do, everything we commit to, takes away the minutes and hours—and ultimately the years—of our lives.

But That's Just Modern Life!

In my own life and business, I have surrounded myself with highly qualified people with the expertise to help my company grow expo-nentially, but most people never take these kinds of extraordinary steps. This is why so many small businesses remain sole proprietor-ships, which is worse than working at a job. It's also one of the main reasons behind the high rate of business failures.

While managing time is really relatively simple, it is *never* easy. But like most other things we've looked at, it's all about choice: How do you choose to use your time? How do the activities of today, of this hour, of this minute, take you closer to your goals?

Sure, there are all sorts of great opportunities all around us . . . but who's got the time?

Your Most Valuable Asset

Time is our most precious, most valuable asset, because no matter what we do, we can't squeeze another second out of our day. We may joke about "working 25-hour days," but that's just wishful thinking.

The more demands we have on our time, the more valuable our time is, or should be.

Unfortunately, we are largely a nation of wage-slaves, living in a world of wage-slaves, all trading hours for dollars. At the end of the run, we often have very few dollars and very few minutes left to enjoy our lives.

Honestly, the whole idea that we should manage our time has only been around for 150 years or so. When folks lived on farms, time management meant getting up at the crack of dawn and feeding the chickens, slopping the hogs, milking the cows, and doing whatever else the animals required. You measured time from sunup to sundown. I'm simplifying their life, but I'm not assuming life was easy.

Wage-Slaves and Keeping Time

As workers started leaving the farms and working in the cities, their pay was calculated according to the number of manufactured items they completed in a day. It was called *piecework* and it was the norm for a long, long time. The standards were always just over what was humanly possible, so the bosses didn't have to pay living wages because the workers "weren't putting out enough product."

Finally, Henry Ford introduced the "minimum" wage of $5 a day, not too shabby at the time. People truly began to trade hours for dollars, and continue this today. Because people were paid for time, the efficient use of time became very important. Soon every workplace was undergoing efficiency studies. The more efficient, the better the bottom line profit. The less efficient, the less profit. Efficiency measured output per man-hour, and we were back to a new kind of piecework.

The very term *time management* assumes people can manage something that can't be stopped, can't be controlled. Time marches on. The only thing we can manage is ourselves and how we *use* the minutes and hours, even seconds, of our day. So we're back to where we started from: it's up to us to allot the amount of time we spend or waste; and once we use it, we cannot, ever, get it back or reuse the time. Is your time worth managing?

*I value time. I refuse to waste my time. So I manage
my time so I get to have more time to enjoy my life.*

It's hard to overestimate the value of managing your own time. After all, if you can't manage yourself, how can you ever hope to manage others? If you can't manage others, how can you advance in your career? If you allow yourself weak excuses, how can you have any integrity demanding more of the people who report to you (or will, assuming you intend to go for the goal).

*You may make a living from 8 to 5, but you make a
life from 5 o'clock on.*

You'll never get rich working for someone else. There's a mind shift we all have to go through: How much do we value our time? What are you *really* worth? How much are your hours worth to you? How much is your free time worth? If you measure yourself by whatever you're being paid now, you're missing my point.

Let me put it another way: Let's say you have a chance to do some side work, some consulting, doing what you do right now. How much could you straight-faced, look-em-in-the-eye, ask to be paid for your work? Not how much most people charge for the same kind of work in the marketplace. How much are you worth? How much?

This is a difficult concept for people who've been raised thinking about hours for dollars, dollars for hours. The way you value your own time will determine the value you put on those minutes and hours of each day. And once you get this thought, you will never be the same.

How Do I Squeeze Extra Minutes Out of My Busy Day?

The first thing to get hold of is exactly what your goals are. This is the sum and substance of this whole book: ***Figure out what you want and write it down.*** Next, figure out how to ***prioritize your time,*** how to maximize what you've got to do, and finally, how to ***delegate as much as possible.*** Delegation is one of the most difficult steps because it taps into trust issues.

Figure Out What You Want and Write It Down

My mom still remembers when I came home from school, sometime around the time I was 10 or 11, with this goal book I'd written. It was probably some class assignment, but for me it was real. I figured if I put something down in that goal book, it was going to happen.

Someone said the difference between dreams and goals is that goals are written. I don't know about that, but I do know this: ***What gets written, gets done.*** If you're serious about your goals, commit them to paper. Write them down because they're your road map to success. And go the extra step of putting timelines on them. It's amazing how that one piece of added commitment makes so much difference.

> *If you don't know where you're going, any old road will get you there.*

Most students I talk to say they already know what they want. When I ask them how many have a clear plan on how they'll achieve what they want, I still get quite a few hands. How many have written it down? One or two hands, sometimes none. Even if they have a goal, the majority of people really have no plan to achieve it except by some vague concept of going to school, getting their degree, and working hard.

Successful people make lists constantly, every day. It's the only way they can stay on top of their goals and priorities and know where they stand at any given moment. It also allows them to visually see what steps have been completed or not and be very flexible if they see a need to change priorities.

Yearly goals should be reviewed every day, and weekly or monthly goals should be adjusted as needed to make sure you hit your marks. The same is true for your personal and business goals as well. If not, you'll find yourself getting sidetracked, majoring in minor, unproductive activities, and mustering only minor focus when it comes to the major things that you need to do to reach your goal.

> Without a vision, the people perish.
>
> *—Proverbs 29:18*

I've continuously set newer and higher goals along the way and written them down. Then, I went after them. I told friends and family and others about them, but I didn't let them talk me out of my dreams or let ridicule slow me down. Starting a job search company for teens, finding ways to help churches get more return on their investments, helping communities and working class families, raising serious investment money for my companies, taking a company public . . . all of these have been spoken, written, focused goals.

There are all sorts of different formulas for creating goals. One is the SMART goal approach that says your goals should be *Specific, Measurable, Attainable, Realistic, and Time-based.* Another refers to the ABCs: Goals should be *Achievable, Believable, and Controllable.*

Set Real Goals

First, you have to believe the goal is something you can get in the time frame you are aiming at. Otherwise, you're all blow and no go. If all you've ever earned is minimum wage, beating Bill Gates to become the wealthiest person in the world over the next five years isn't a believable goal to anyone, yourself included. So when I look at my goals, I ask myself these questions:

- *Is this goal believable?* Do you know what it takes to make $100,000 a year? $8,334 a month? $1,923 a week? It's less than $50 an hour, if you're talking a 40-hour week. Still sounds like a lot? It's $25 an hour at 80 hours. Eighty hours is a lot to put in, but it goes fast when it's your own thing. The point is: Can you believe that you can make $25 to $50 an hour? How much do you *believe* you can make?

- *Is this goal attainable?* Being able to do it goes hand-in-hand with believing you can do it. Wanting to become a princess isn't a goal unless you were born into royalty. Becoming president isn't a goal if you weren't born in the United States. Just ask Arnold Schwarzenegger. He made it to governor, but president is out of the question unless the rules change. If you've never run for office and getting into politics is on your list, go for the school board or city council, or even neighborhood watch captain first—then governor.

- *Is this goal measurable?* Like I mentioned earlier. Wanting a lot of money isn't a goal. Wanting $100,000 a year—or even $1 million—is better, but it still needs to be broken down to become effective. Want to learn piano or go to art school? When do you plan to start? When do you plan to reach the goal? What's your measuring stick? What are your benchmarks for success? How do you know if you're on track or not? If you don't break it down into smaller, measurable pieces, you'll get to October and be $80,000 shy of your goal. This step lets you see how you're doing all along the way.

By the same token, if you're in April and you're over halfway to your goal, why not bump up the target a bit? Make it $125,000 by the end of the year, or make it $100,000 by August. You can always achieve more if that's what you want.

Goals Must Be Written Down and a Time Limit Set

I've already touched on written goals, and it's true for long-term goals such as retirement, right down to short-range goals such as covering the rent by the twentieth of the month, or paying an extra $50 a month on your credit card balances.

When we don't have any clear goals and priorities, with specific objectives and timelines, we end up taking on too many things—and all of them were due yesterday. It creates crisis management, where all we seem to do is put out fires. And that steals even more of our valuable time!

Prioritize Your Goals

Once you've figured out what you want, the next step is to put those goals into some kind of order, to figure out which ones are the most important to work toward first.

For example, if the rent is due and you're out of work, looking for a job might take priority over going to college full-time. But if going to school and getting a particular degree or training is your long-term goal, start night classes or take some online classes until you can afford to go full-time. If getting your own fashion designs out there into stores is a priority item, learning jazz saxophone might take a back burner for a while.

A lot of people struggle with prioritizing their goals, and end up bouncing around without really focusing on getting the job done. Instead of enjoying accomplishments along the way, they feel inadequate or overwhelmed. The first step in prioritizing is to evaluate honestly how you spend your day right now.

Step One: Evaluation

This is one of the hardest steps in the process, because honesty and accuracy are necessary, just like with a financial budget. Do you sometimes get to three or four o'clock in the afternoon and wonder where the day went? Does Sunday night come and you've only gotten a few of the things done that you wanted to accomplish over the weekend?

Grab an old school planner or a notepad where you can jot down notes on events, commute times, phone calls, tasks, interruptions, shopping, dining, Web surfing, e-mail reading and answering, chilling out, watching television, sleeping, and all the other minutes of the day. And I do mean minutes. Get as precise as you can, so you can add up where your time goes.

This is just for you. Do this for a couple of weeks. Keep a "Captain's Log," like on Star Trek. Until you do this, you'll be living a lie, believing that you don't have any time.

After a couple of weeks of this drudgery, start adding up the minutes and hours. Being a computer geek, I put stuff like this in a spreadsheet, but you can do it on a napkin by hand if you want. The key is, how many minutes or hours do you spend on all these things, these tasks, these events? How much of the 168 hours each week did you spend asleep? How much time yakking on the phone? How much was drive time? You get the idea.

Now how much time is left? That's your starting point. Ground zero. This is the time you have already, right now, every week, to pursue your dream.

I've never met anyone who did this who wasn't shocked at how much time they DID have. But this is just the beginning. It's a tough beginning, but we have to do it to prove to ourselves that **we *do* have time.**

Something else a lot of people realize is that they've spread themselves too thin. They feel that they have to accomplish everything yesterday and don't give themselves enough time to do things properly. This leads only to half-finished projects and no feeling of achievement. Good news. The way to avoid this *and* squeeze more out of the hours of our day is the simplest part of the process:

Step Two: Prioritize
This is where we start assigning individual short-term goals (the baby steps) to the different long-term goals (the big accomplishments) in our life.

> *Essentially, our lives are made up of I-have-tos,*
> *I-feel-obligated-tos, drop-everything-and-dos and*
> *I-wanna-dos.*

"Have-tos" include things like cleaning the house, grocery shopping, completing job assignments, and taking care of our kids. Commuting to work—I saw a news report that the average commute time is 51 minutes a day. Even though we make the decisions about where we live and work, it's still a "have-to" reality. And yes, "have-tos" can include our "honey-dos," at least if we want to keep our relationships on a even keel.

We have the least control of the things in the "have-to" category, but, using our ability to manage our time, we can still squeeze a few hours from here, too.

"I-feel-obligated-tos" can include a lot of things we say yes to but groan inside about. Or we feel like we have to do them because nobody else will. Jobs at work end up on our desk, or we find ourselves volunteering for diaper duty at church one Sunday "Because they were short of helpers," and three years later we're doing the Nursery every service, missing out on our own growth in the process. There's a simple solution to these time-stealing activities:

Just say "No!"

Sometimes the best time management skill we can pick up is to say no to extra errands, more responsibilities at work, volunteering with clubs or organizations, or whatever. If people think they can dump their load on your shoulders, they will. Some of the most stressed people I know are so concerned they won't be liked or that they'll upset someone, they have a hard time just saying "No." We need to screen every request for the minutes of our time, and use our overall goals and objectives as our measuring stick.

Ask yourself: "Is this the best use of my time?" If not, say "No." Let someone else share the burden. Give others the opportunity to carry their weight, and don't do everything for them. Every church, every organization, every company has a few people who seem to be Everyman or Everywoman. They can do all sorts of things that may be needed, and they have a hard time not "helping" when asked. Their helping doesn't usually help, not because they don't get the job done, but because someone else missed the chance to learn the process and share responsibility. The organization doesn't get stronger—it gets weaker, and more dependent on that one person. What happens if they get sick? Just saying no will often have the effect of making things better, not worse, because others will learn to pick up the slack.

Don't confuse this with being a team member and doing what-ever it takes to succeed. If volunteering a certain number of hours each week is part of your goals (and it *is* part of my own), then do it; just don't let others assume that because you're willing and able that your time is up for grabs for any and everything that needs to be done.

Do give back to your community, your house of worship, and other charities, but manage your giving time as well. This is about understanding your goals and objectives, and not getting derailed by other things.

I challenge you to look carefully at this category
because for most people just learning to say "No" can
buy them the extra time they need to succeed.

"Drop-everything-and-dos" are the things that come out of nowhere, because we didn't take the time to handle it right in the beginning. As my mom would say, "People don't have time to do things right, but they always have time to do them over." When you're up to your neck in alligators, it's easy to forget the objective was to drain the swamp. Peter Drucker says, "Crisis management is actually the form of management preferred by most managers." Why? It's easier to put off until tomorrow what should be done today. Today! Remember? The irony is that this doesn't result in feeling successful; it makes us constantly feel frustrated by our shortcomings and failures.

"I-wanna-dos" are the areas we have the most control over. You wanna watch football every Sunday instead of working on your business plan? Maybe you wanna use it for exercise and hobbies, for time with your family, to play softball, or do barbeques every weekend with your buddies. You wanna go out to eat every night instead of fixing a quick meal and saving time (and money). Every one of the items in this category you have 100 percent control over.

Our "I-wanna-do" time includes our downtime and empty time. We all need a rest. But most of us need a whole lot less resting than we take. We're not an obese nation because we're working too hard and not spending enough "downtime." Look at the way you use your spare time and how it propels—or delays—you from reaching your goal.

I am constantly trying to find new ways to use the empty, wasted time in my life. I sit in a lot of airports and ride in a lot of taxicabs. I have my Blackberry so I can handle calls and e-mails. My laptop allows me to work on other projects. I carry a briefcase with papers to review. I know people who listen to motivational, self-help and business training CDs during their drive time.

Where Is the Time for Me?
Someone's gonna say "I'm no robot. I need my own time. Sounds like you want me to fill every minute with 'productive' stuff. **What about quality time?"**

Our family and friends can be a powerful support group, so plan time with them in your daily schedule. I have my family time right on my company calendar, where all my employees can see where I am. Wednesday night, MeShelle and I and our kids are in church. Don't schedule something for me then, because that time is set aside for my family. When all the success you want has been achieved, these are the people you'll be looking at. And hopefully they'll all be looking back with love and great memories of someone who cared enough to set aside time for them.

Other than managing your own minutes and hours better and saying "No" whenever possible, the surest way to help you get more out of your day is to learn to delegate some of the responsibilities to others. After all, who said it all needs to be on your shoulders?

Delegate as Much as Possible

You aren't the best person to do all the stuff you do right now. It's rare I meet anyone who doesn't have someone else in their life they can delegate some of their tasks to. It can be your children (John, wash the clothes; Sally, put up the dishes). It can be a coworker you share part of a project with, or even a superior in your company who is better equipped to do part of a task. Break bigger tasks into the smaller parts. Break up ongoing jobs (distributing company mail, taking out the trash) between different people. Most important, learn to do this now, so that when you are managing people later on, you'll be able to *manage* them, and not do their jobs for them.

Perfection Is Paralysis

People who are perfectionists are lousy delegators. If a project isn't going the way they think it should, or being done the way they would do it, they'll jump right back in so it's "done right." Let your people mess up. Let them fail. Then use it as part of the learning process. If you think someone else can do something at least 60 percent as good as you, delegate it. And if he can't, then take the time—ONE time— to show him. And have him make notes and e-mail you his notes. For regular jobs (how to fax multiple copies or what to do if you're out of printing supplies), use the notes to start a Standard Operating Procedures (SOP) Manual. That way, you never have to explain it again (a long-term solution for a long-term problem).

The best managers are the ones who are good at delegating work to their staff, and making sure it's done correctly. Delegating doesn't mean you aren't ultimately responsible. It's not a way to pass the buck. Delegating is probably the best way of building your team's morale and sense of pride of ownership. Plus, you cut your workload and other people gain valuable experience. Everyone wins!

Don't allow anyone to take your time from you.

Be jealous of the minutes of your life. Set some clear boundaries, for instance, if someone stops you in the hall to discuss some project, ask her if she can get back to you at a certain time, to set an appointment basically, so you can schedule in the time just for her. Don't allow coworkers to highjack your time. I've read the average manager spends 17 hours a week, just in meetings. Other studies have shown that meetings eat up half your typical manager's time each week, or more. And it doesn't end there. They spend another hour or so every day, planning and preparing for the meetings, and even more afterwards, in the different follow-ups with staff. Patrick Lencioni showed us all the cures for "death by meeting" in his book by that name. It's one of my favorites, Emerson's too, and a must read for anyone thinking about super success.

Insanity is when you keep on doing the same things,
hoping for different results.

Managing our time gives us the freedom to pursue the things we really want most in life. Not managing our time keeps us living in mediocrity, poverty, and dependent on others (the company, the boss, the government) to take care of us—if not now, then in the days ahead. Not managing our time gives others the power to control the minutes and seconds, hours and days, weeks and months and years of our lives to others. It makes it easier to be cast about on every wave with no compass to guide us and no chart or map to follow to move ahead and rise above.

Ephesians 5:16 says, "Redeem the time, because the days are evil." Other translations word it more like, "Make the most of your time and opportunities." Because all the distractions and interruptions and things that have to get done in your life will steal away your time if you don't start managing them.

The day we start managing our time is the day we begin giving ourselves time to enjoy, really enjoy, life. Manage your time wisely. You and your dreams are worth it.

Excuse Number Three: I Don't Have an Education

I hear this excuse a lot from young people, but it applies to all ages: "I'm not educated enough to start and run a business." I believe education is meant to broaden your horizons, open up new worlds and new understandings about the world and the people in it. The primary purpose of higher education is not to equip you to make a million dollars. Get an education, but separate the notion that your education is going to make you successful. It will enrich your life, but success is up to you.

There are literally hundreds of millionaires in the business world, myself included, who either never set foot in a college classroom or dropped out after realizing that college wasn't going to take them where they wanted to go.

- Ever hear of a man named Ray Kroc? He was the founder and CEO of one of the largest restaurant chains in the world, McDonalds. Even though he founded "Hamburger University," he never spent a day in college.
- You've probably never heard of Kemmons Wilson but you have definitely heard of Holiday Inns. Mr. Wilson was the founder of Holiday Inns and, by the time he sold out, probably a billionaire; yet, he didn't even graduate from high school.
- Here's another brand name you'll recognize: Coca Cola. Did you know the man who headed the world's most famous soft drink company in the 1900s, Charles E. Culpepper, never attended a university?

These are all ordinary people who had faith and belief in their abilities and didn't let the lack of higher education get in the way.

They found other ways to get the knowledge they needed and paved their own road to success.

> Schooling is what happens inside the wall of the school, some of which is educational. Education happens everywhere, and it happens from the moment a child is born—some say before— until it dies.
>
> —*Sara Lawrence Lightfoot*

I'm really not anti-education, but I am pretty down on the current educational model we use in this country. I believe the education system as it's structured now is just antiquated. A degree is an extra credential that people look at and say, "Oh, he's got a degree so he must know something." But I can't tell you how many of the people we've hired with all these degrees are complete morons. They have no understanding, no common sense, and a lot of the time no people skills at all. They want to get paid for their degrees, but an employer wants to pay based on performance, based on results. *What have you done for me lately?*

Our concept of what makes "education" is pretty new. We didn't even have compulsory education laws in the United States until 1852, when Massachusetts required that everyone from 8 to 14 attend school at least three months each year. Even then, they didn't have to go if they could show they knew the material. So the first laws about public schooling based attendance on individual competency. What went wrong? No other state followed Massachusetts until 15 years later, after the Civil War. Bet you had no idea that it took until 1933—66 years and a couple of wars later (see, you weren't thinking about the Spanish-American War in there, now were you? Back to your history books!)—before all 48 states had compulsory education.

In my opinion, we've created theoretical training systems and allowed the children of this country to be guinea pigs, locked into compulsory schools with burned-out teachers, learning dry book knowledge with nothing to relate it to in their lives. They don't go to school to learn at all, just to stay off the street and out of our hair. They go to school to memorize . . . and to pass tests.

The latest incarnation of these programs is the "No Child Left Behind" Act. It almost guarantees that teachers spend most of their time "teaching to the test," so the *school* doesn't get a bad grade. Looks like we've basically given up on meaningful education for individuals altogether.

> Don't let your schooling get in the way of your education.
>
> —*Mark Twain*

Getting an education has come to mean certain things today that are a whole lot different than the way people in the past thought about the process. For most of history, nobody figured that going to college was necessarily the *key* requirement to be successful. Contrary to the popular saying, **knowledge is NOT power.**

Only *Applied* Knowledge Is Power—And You Can't Apply It if You're Sitting in a Classroom

I went to college for about a year but literally had to drop out because of responsibilities with my company. But I maintained a 3.8 GPA without ever opening my books. It just became an issue of, "Gee, do I focus on building a multimillion-dollar company, or do I focus on getting this elective checked off so I can take the next class and get a sheepskin?" How long do you think I had to think about that?

I just think people are individuals, but our compulsory education system treats everyone the same. You need 180 days in class to learn this. You need 1 hour and 15 minutes in each class. You need multiple choice standardized tests. Do I? *Really?*

Education exposes us to knowledge and information resources. It's up to us to use them to our advantage. "Getting an education" does not by default mean "go to college." It *can* mean this, but it really means we need to thirst for the knowledge and information and acquire it through every means and resource we can use.

Keep your eyes on the prize. If you don't have a clear-cut goal in mind, all the training, education, and knowledge won't mean a thing. And if you don't apply the knowledge you gain, no matter where it comes from, it will just sit there dormant, worthless in your life.

> *I didn't go for a college degree, but that doesn't*
> *mean I didn't get an education.*

This was a big argument with my parents, especially my dad. Big argument. Huge. I brought all these books home to read and study to become proficient in programming. Read them myself, in my room, until I understood what they were saying.

It was Dad, remember, who drilled it into my head to "Go to school, get a job." I'd use Bill Gates right back at him, and tell him Gates never went to college. Look at him and what all he's done. Didn't seem to hurt him much.

I bought Richard Kiyosaki's book, *Rich Dad, Poor Dad* (New York: Time Warner, 2002) to show my dad how the whole time and money thing worked. Taking years to get started just didn't make sense to me. I couldn't see me doing that, not with one multimillion-dollar business already in the bag, and even bigger dreams and goals besides. His dad had drilled into his head that education was "better to have and not need, than to need and not have." Man, did we go round and round.

Finally, I applied at several different colleges, and even got accepted at a college in California and one in Chicago, I also did some courses at Baker University, right in Overland Park, as well as some other courses online. But I was focused on my goal. I'll never forget when Dad took me up to Chicago to sign the papers at Columbia University, for their high-tech computer school where I had been accepted. I changed my mind literally at the registration table. My mom says, "Ephren turned down all the colleges and all he wanted to do was computers. Later he needed all these certifications and wanted to go through the Microsoft training, which was like a crash course."

My heart was set on doing this specialized Microsoft training Mom and Dad called "Bill Gates U." It was $15,000. Once my folks realized how determined I was, Dad put up the tuition so I could go.

He knew I had been reading technical manuals myself since I was 12 years old. He realized how serious I was.

We have to learn to chart our own course or we'll be constantly moved and pushed where other people want us to be. The result of my parents' decision to support my goal? I became the youngest tech ever to complete all of the required certification levels.

Rosella A. Sprow, principal of Roche World Group (www .rocheworldgroup.com) works with City Capital on our grants and funding. I recently asked her to head up our special projects division at our Goshen Energy subsidiary. Rosella has a great vision, especially for historically black colleges and universities (HBCUs) around the country. She is also a modern mom and says:

> As the mother of a seven year-old, I have been inspired by Mr. Taylor
> to look at the way I groom my son. I no longer think of the traditional
> approach to higher education as—go to college and see what you can
> make happen from there. I realize it is my responsibility to encourage,
> expose, and empower him during his formative years so that he can
> create his own professional plan and cultivate the leader within. I will
> still save for college, but if he shows any of the discipline, insight, and
> commitment to success for a business idea as did Mr. Taylor, I would
> seriously consider investing in his effort and allowing him to take busi-
> ness and management classes on the side.

Yes, you need an education. You probably don't need as much as you think. Too often, extending our education beyond a certain point is simply a crutch, not for the added knowledge we'll get, but for added security or confidence, or some other inner needs. Passion and focus will carry you a long way toward your success. Make sure you have the knowledge you really need, and the education you really need, but don't think you have to wait around years to get started.

Even though I didn't complete college, I get invited to speak to college business classes all the time. I'm invited as a business and community development expert to speak on national panels such as the Congressional Black Caucus in Washington, DC. I get calls from radio and television newsrooms for commentary on events, and articles are written in every city where I'm invited to speak on our Urban Wealth Tour.

Poor Communication Skills

Over the years I've had partners, even adults, ask me to make presentations or speak for them. I'm not talking about the people who are afraid to stand up in front of a room, who have a fear of failure. (We'll cover that in the next section.) Here I'm talking about people who feel like they, "sound too ignorant to talk to people." Or their "English isn't good enough."

Is your excuse that you have a thick accent, or that you don't speak very well and never mastered all the rules of grammar? Let's look at how an accent may or may not be a handicap for you. It might make you self-conscious when talking to some people but is it really a problem?

Immigrants from all over the world come to the United States with no practical knowledge of our language. Yet they start businesses and prosper. I've mentioned Arnold Schwarzenegger already. He was just a muscleman from Austria with an accent so thick it was really hard to understand him in the early days, but he became famous as an actor and eventually was elected the governor of California. He's just one example of someone who didn't let their English, or their speaking skills, stop them from succeeding.

This Ain't a Ticket to Slide

It goes without saying that you should have adult-level reading skills, no matter what it takes to get there. That way, you can do research and find the information you need, and read and understand it when you get it. You should be able to pick up a business report or prospectus and understand 90 percent of the words—or know where to find the definitions of the ones you don't.

Any person who wants to succeed in business, art, music, or anything else should also know how to communicate in decent English. Understanding good grammar and being able to string together complete sentences, I mean, this is basic stuff.

If you have reached high school graduation age or beyond and you still don't have these kinds of basic literacy and math skills, my friend, you have some catching up to do. I'd suggest you knuckle down and take remedial classes, go back and re-read your high school textbooks or find a mentor who will teach you. While you're at it, learn how to write a good business letter and how to add a column of figures. It's not up to your teachers or parents or anyone else but you because it's your goals on the line.

There's No Excuse to Speak in Uneducated Slang

Don't even go there. If you think urban gangsta ought to be how everyone talks, or think mumbling answers is cool, think again. If you're just a "po' ol' country boy," plan on people treating you like one. If you figure people better just learn to get it when you talk—like it's their problem, not yours—you're out of the game already.

Prejudice means *pre*-judging, and our speech is one of the primary things people use to judge us. You can get upset about it, get an attitude that it's their problem, not yours. You can rant and bellyache about being "genuine," but it won't change things. If you want to play "code-shifting" at home, fine. Leave the slang and mumbling street talk there. It's human nature to categorize or prejudge people. We all do it. You do it too. You can accept it and use it to your advantage, or you get run over by it.

You ever notice how movies and television always make the character with a Southern drawl stupid, or a con or used car salesman type? I mean, come on! Tom Hanks isn't from the South. They didn't cast him as Forrest Gump with a Boston or British accent! Part of why he sounded dumb was because he spoke in a slow, drawling accent. If you haven't paid attention to how language typecasts people, start now. Do you hear a deep South accent and immediately think "redneck"? What other terms come into your mind?

How does the media portray urban black kids? How does urban slang or urban dress work for business? When someone uses a lot of "dees" and "dos," or "youse guys" or "ya'lls," or "yo" and "whassup," what kinds of images does it bring to your mind? Not someone I'd be voting into office. Sounds too much like a good ol' boy, homie, or a street hood to trust them.

Or it may just sound plain ignorant and low-rate. You can hang all the tags you want off your Polo shirts, and lean way over to pump up your Jordan's where everyone can see your bling hanging down, but it sends the message that you're impressed with yourself, and that you figure everyone oughta just take you or leave you. Well guess what, you're outta here! That hole in your foot and in your wallet is from your own bullet, not the Man's.

This is one area where study and training are important. The good news is, you can find English language tapes and CDs in the local library, so "not being able to communicate" is no excuse.

I know what I'm talking about here. I grew up in an educated family, but all my friends talked that trash talk all day long—*All day long.* I've done my share of code-shifting along the way. Does that make me fake? Disingenuous? Not "authentic"? I had to learn to speak and act in a way that my ideas and vision would be listened to. I've been told this is selling out, that I'm not "authentically black," whatever that means, by black friends and even family. It's no different from the white kids in my high school thinking all black kids played basketball! It's no different. I'll say this a hundred times, our perception is our reality.

Emerson Brantley was born in the South, raised in the South, schooled in the South. Most of his family was from Georgia. Some of them talk with a Geechee accent so thick, he can hardly understand them himself. He can pour on a Southern accent, but you know what? You'd bet your paycheck he was from upstate New York or somewhere in the Midwest. He knows how to talk properly and use correct English.

My wife MeShelle grew up in the Kansas City hood, but she doesn't talk (or dress) like a street girl. She has education and culture and insists on excellence. She hasn't sold out; she's recognized that some speech patterns indicate lower class, or even ignorance, and cloud any opportunity from the get-go. Why would anybody choose to stack the deck against themselves? ***There is no cultural pride in being or acting ignorant.*** There is no cultural gain by promoting a culture of failure. There is nothing genuine about looking and sounding like a loser. And there sure isn't anything in my heritage that would say any different.

When You're in Someone Else's House, You Play by Their Rules

Learning to speak the language of business is what I call playing by the house rules. If you want to enter a contract, sell a painting, open a business, make a presentation, or whatever, it's up to you to communicate in ways the other person understands.

If you come to my house and we play Monopoly, nobody gets to win the Free Parking money (which are the real rules anyway). It doesn't matter if that's not how you've always played it at your house. You can play the game, but you've got to follow the rules I play by in my house. And like the lottery ads say, "If you don't play, you can't win." So it's your choice, but don't expect me to change my rules just because you don't like them. That's not my job. It's your job to adapt.

Excuse Number Four: I Don't Have Enough Information and Knowledge

A lot of times when people say they don't have enough education, they're really saying they don't have the **knowledge** they feel they need to succeed in whatever the field is they've chosen. This excuse really feeds heavily into our fear of failure. Honest, hardworking people can become immobilized with feelings of inadequacy, especially when confronting unfamiliar details on a complex project. I have seen investors literally freeze up, unwilling to take a step in *any* direction when it comes to making a decision about their investing at all because of a real—or perceived—lack of knowledge.

So instead of trying to make significant gains—*playing to win*—some people seem overcome by the paralysis of analysis they play *not to lose*, in a futile attempt to personally gain every tiny piece of knowledge and information available before making a decision. And so they never make one until the opportunity has passed them by.

But if I don't have the time to understand all the ins and outs of a business, how can I ever get enough experience to do it profitably . . . and not worry about losing money?

While knowledge itself is simple enough to attain, acquiring it is not necessarily an easy activity to fit into our already busy lives. It requires not just spare time, but focused, prioritized quality time to gain understanding. The good news is knowledge can be obtained, and more information resources are available to teach business strategies and techniques today than ever before.

I have been approached more than once by a business broker to buy businesses. Often, they are multimillion-dollar companies, but because they haven't adapted to changes in the market, they are usually losing money big time by the time they reach my desk. If I can see how we could potentially mesh our business model with theirs, and if they have developed good contacts in their market, I'll make an offer.

Do I have all the knowledge to make it work? No. But I know that with the right numbers in the deal, by changing their marketing model or some other parts of their business structure, we can probably turn them around to profitability. I trust my instincts, my own decisions. You don't have to have every piece of information to make a decision. Period. Decide the bare minimum you must have and go with it. Don't cut off the flow of facts and information; be willing to change and adapt as you need to, to adjust to changes in your market.

> One thing is sure. We have to do something. We have to do the best we know how at the moment. If it doesn't turn out right, we can modify it as we go along.
>
> —*Franklin D. Roosevelt*

My commonsense approach has always been that there is just no way I can possibly know everything I need to know in advance to allow me to jump on every opportunity that comes along. I'm only one person, but this doesn't mean I don't want to take advantage of deals that come my way. I simply don't believe in depending on my personal knowledge and expertise alone. The good news is, there are lots of other experts out there with specialized training.

Find People Who Have "Been There, Done That"

You don't have to know everything. As long as there are other experts and professionals we can rely on who understand the deal structure and can give us the guidance we need, count me in. That's the power of multiplying expertise and efforts to achieve quantum results.

From my earliest business experience, I have sought out and gathered specific experts in different fields to create a knowledgeable, aggressive team. This human infrastructure can handle many types of opportunities . . . real estate, mortgages, stocks, oil and gas, absentee businesses, commercial developments, mergers and acquisitions, land consolidation, and others. We have dedicated contractors, appraisers, lawyers, marketing experts, and other specialists to guide us and carry out the details for the follow through.

What Are You Waiting For?

How old are you right now? 30? 40? 60? 12? Lots of people find it surprising that I began focusing on business at the tender age of 12. That's when most kids are riding bicycles, playing video games, and basically fooling around. Nobody's serious at age 12, right? Maybe everyone else thought that way, but obviously I didn't.

I loved video games. I loved them so much I could pretty much master every one I got my hands on pretty quickly. Still can. By the time I was 12, my parents were fed up with shelling out money for my games, and wouldn't buy me this one new game I wanted. My dad basically told me if it was that important, to go figure out how to make one myself. So that's what I did.

I played lots of video games but I sure didn't have any experience programming them—I was only 12! So I went to the best sources of information I could find (and that I could afford, like the library), and I figured out how to do it. Taught myself. Our family didn't even have a computer at the time. I had to use the ones at school.

Later on, I bought my own books from some of my profits, and even took some programming courses. But in the beginning, I hit the free information at the library. Today, when I talk to college or high school classes, I call this my *Knowledge Expansion Program.* There's a tremendous amount of information you can get from books, but you have to be a self-starting learner. You can't expect someone to just hand it to you.

I studied hard, I worked on my programming after school, and found mentors to guide me. I didn't have a college degree or even a high school diploma. I just did it. I created my own game! Pretty soon I figured out I could make $10 for burning CDs and selling my game to other kids. Flame Software was born, and I was in a very profitable business almost before I knew it. Was I too young to do that? Of course not! I just did it! Are you too young—or too old—to start a business? I don't think so. Is someone else going to do it for you or just hand it to you? Do you even need to ask?

Whatever It Takes

I kept going. By age 16, I had won Microsoft's Teen TechFest Challenge, and had started a job search engine for teens. I was building a business, raising money, and putting together agreements with Wal-Mart, Citigroup, Sprint, Target, the Air National Guard, and others. I got them to list their jobs on my search engine. Oh, and keeping up with my math and science and English homework at the same time.

The Kauffman Center for Entrepreneurial Leadership is in Kansas City, and I heard about their EntrePrep scholarship so I applied for it and won. By winning that scholarship, I was able to attend the Kauffman Center, and the things I learned at Kauffman took me to a whole new level and helped me build my business skills even more.

I picked up some more mentors along the way. They taught me about growing a business, hiring, managing, preparing myself, and making presentations to investors to raise money and a whole lot more. That was how I was able to personally raise over $250,000 to grow my company.

And man, did we grow it! GoFerretGo.com grew into a company worth millions by the time I was 17. By 19, I retired, and started helping my dad in a church he'd started. I took the donation and endowment monies and started managing them, investing them into homes for families within our own community. I used all the things I had learned up until that point to develop some winning investment strategies that earned me Kansas Young Entrepreneur of the Year in 2002. I've kept on refining those strategies and we still use them in our companies today. Plus a few more I've picked up along the way.

What *Is* the Right Time to Get Serious and Get Moving toward Your Goals?

Is there a right or wrong time to start thinking about a moneymaking career? How about right now? Today? Not tomorrow, not once you get over this or that problem or finish doing this thing or the other. But today. We don't have any promises about tomorrow, but we do have today. Now what are we going to do with it?

We've already talked about how Conventional Wisdom says you get your education first, then enter the business world, start at the bottom and work hard, and you'll rise to the top. The rest of the message is kind of vague. Success just sort of happens. But for most "worker bees" out there, what has this line of reasoning reinforced?

I believe most people have been conditioned to work for someone else, to trade hours for dollars and become dependent on someone else for their income. It's been said the epitaph of an average man or woman should read something like this:

> *Average Man or Woman*
> *Rest in Peace*
> *Born 1950*
> *Died 1968*
> *Buried 2008*

Look. If all you want is a good, safe, steady job and income, okay. If the risk of owning your own business, being your own boss, and making financial decisions is way outside of your comfort zone, don't do it. But don't count on your needs or wants being of any consequence to the company you work for. We all know people who have spent years as loyal, dedicated employees, only to have the company they poured their life into cut staff, increase responsibilities, raid their retirement plan, and ultimately lay them off or fire them along with hundreds or thousands of others.

Again, none of this is meant to bash a "traditional" career path, but I will throw this at you: Why wait? Why not do both? Why does anyone have to wait until [they finish school, get married, have kids, whatever] before they go for it? Why can't a person be in business for themselves at age 12, 13, 14, or 15? Why can't you go into business today, if that's your dream?

And I encourage you to not accept excuses that might hold you back. How do you define things like *education, knowledge, information, or experience?* Do you accept lockstep the way society currently defines them? Or do your look at what they mean in your life, to your dreams and goals? How you choose to perceive these, and all the other excuses, will determine your destiny. The choice is yours to make.

Excuse Number Five: I Don't Have the Experience

While information and knowledge are necessary ingredients for making quality decisions, experience comes only from *applied* information and knowledge. Hard as it may be to accept, while we can learn a lot from books, CDs, courses and seminars, we can't get experience without getting out there in the trenches and making decisions.

> *Good judgment comes from experience, and experience comes from bad judgment.*

Ouch. You can literally spend tens of thousands of dollars on courses and seminars with real estate "gurus," for example, but if you want to get personal experience investing in real estate, sooner or later, you have to take your chances and actually *buy* a property, and learn the process hands on. **That's experience.** You buy your ticket and you take your chance.

Value of Experience

There is very little evidence that there is any great personal value in having experience in every detail of a business. The fact is most people accept this in other areas of their life without question. Few would try to do a legal transaction without an attorney, for example. While we may gain some new experiences each time, we aren't generally assuming that we can possibly know enough of the intricacies of the law to be our own attorney. You've been seeing doctors for years. Are you ready to self-diagnose that serious illness you can't seem to shake?

How many go to mechanic school so they can drive their car? We jump in, plug in the key, and throw it into gear. Do you even *know* how a dual-overhead cam 24-valve engine with electronic fuel injection works? Do you care, as long as it gets you there? Most of us are lucky if we know where the gas nozzle goes, and where the battery terminals are in case we need a jump. So why do we think we need to have all the experience and understanding to start a particular business?

Michael Gerber, in *The E-Myth Revisited* (New York: HarperCollins, 1995) calls this the "Fatal Assumption." According to Gerber, we assume that if we understand the technical work of a business, we understand the business that does that technical work. And it just isn't true. In fact, he goes so far as to suggest we should *avoid* businesses we think we have a good understanding about or experience in or those that we "like" or are "good at" (he uses the example of a woman who started a bakery because she was a good cook).

You don't need a lot of experience to recognize the needs of the marketplace. You don't need to be an engineer to come up with a basic design or concept. The fact is you can hire professionals for all of the gaps in your knowledge base, and you can focus on—and get paid for—being the visionary, the entrepreneur, the dealmaker.

Part of the problem with getting experience is that our educational system sometimes stands in the way.

I touched on this in the section about the excuse of needing more education to succeed. Over the past 100 years or so, our educational system has given us very narrow "modern" definitions of what education, information, and knowledge all mean today. *And our ability to get real-world experience is tied into this rigid formula.*

If you're locked down in school eight hours a day, if your time after school is filled with sports and activities and all sorts of "play," then where do you find the time to get the experience you need to succeed?

Over the past century, there were a lot of movements and discussions and referendums about children, education, child labor, and child welfare. And not all of these were really concerned about the welfare of the children at all. There was something else going on there.

In the Past, Kids Got All the Experience They Could Handle, and Then Some

Young people and adults had always worked together. A kid couldn't pull as much weight as an adult, but nobody ever thought a kid shouldn't be encouraged to work. Even today, kids around the world help support their families and their communities. Apprenticeship programs and other on-the-job learning takes place every day. In America, we look on all that as ignorant and old school. Modern education locks kids up five days a week and expect them to play the rest of the time. Now *that's* intelligent. Our system doesn't give kids much room to do anything but "get educated." What if a kid like me has other ideas? Our system doesn't have a lot of room for nonconforming kids. It's basically one-size-fits-all.

During the Great Depression—when basically, America went broke—skyrocketing unemployment and soup lines sealed the deal. We couldn't have kids competing with adults, regardless of their abilities. Couldn't have a kid taking a man's job away, so the courts decided kids needed "protection." I'm not making light of sweatshop conditions and child abuse on an industrial scale. But if we think all these great advances were made for our children's benefit, we're turning a blind eye to the economic and political changes that created the way things are today.

I read one study that showed teenagers endure almost 10 times as many rules and restrictions as adults and almost twice as many as active-duty Marines serving in Iraq. And get this: *teenagers have twice as many restrictions as convicted, sentenced, felons in federal pens.*

The end result was that our system today practically eliminates kids from ever competing against adults for jobs. We've made sure that kids and teenagers are kept from most opportunities to get working experience until *after* high school. Even today, the jobs most teens can land are low-paying service work like flipping hamburgers, busing tables, cleaning cars, and doing jobs like that.

The Generation Gap

Today our kids live in a bubble, separated from the real world. The day-to-day activities in a kid's life have very little relevance to the things that are day-to-day for their parents. They basically live separate lives from their parents and other adults. Wait. That sounds like a "Generation Gap?" Wow! Where'd that come from? Adults started thinking teenagers were inherently irresponsible, and not only that, "just not ready" for adulthood. You know, like starting a business, having a checking account, signing documents, driving a car . . . working, expanding their horizons, following their dreams.

Kids started thinking their parents were "old school" fuds that just weren't tuned into what was "real." Parents "just didn't get it" and so, we've created separate societies: one for our children, one for ourselves.

Our educational system has created this whole situation, where kids and grownups don't build learning relationships with each other, where they don't trust each other, and where young people have a real hard time getting their foot in the door to get the experience they need.

I'll tell you what saved me from dropping out of high school altogether: Every day at 11:00 they allowed a special class to leave the school to do on-the-job training, real-world training. Experience. Application of the knowledge. And that's where a lot of us just excelled. That's where I was able to be a sweathog, gofer, or you name it for John Vandewalle, one of my first mentors.

That's when I started to figure out "THAT's why I need to know this stuff in school." So I came out of class with a whole different insight and perception of how I can apply this to my life, and to the job that's going to affect the money that goes into my bank account. My attitude went from "What a waste of time," to "The time I'm spending in this class is time I'm investing in my dream."

Getting Experience Is Investing in Your Goals

So often when we're young, we're more concerned about getting some doofus spit paycheck flipping burgers, rather than putting the same effort into getting the kind of experience we need to succeed. I worked 60 to 80 hours a week under John Vandewalle, and I've worked just as hard under some of my other mentors. Hard time. And I soaked up every drop of the knowledge I needed to do what I do today. I didn't think about it as a job, even though all my friends, even some in my family, told me I was stupid for working "for free." Told me he was using me. Hah! I was using *him* to learn what I needed to know and get the experience I needed to succeed.

See how backward Conventional Wisdom can be sometimes? I *knew* what I was doing. I was in the trenches in boardrooms, offices, and places where other 16-year-olds never get into. I was learning business, big business, firsthand. Learning by watching, learning by listening, learning by doing. They would have committed me to a mental institution if I'd told them what I was really thinking: I would have *paid* my mentors for the chance to get in on their knowledge and networks of contacts! And in a sense, I did, through my sweat and efforts in their businesses.

Seek and Ye Shall Find

There are loads of internship programs you can get into, whether in high school or in college, with for-profit companies and with non-profit organizations you can volunteer at. The point is if you *want* experience, it's waiting for you. Heck, if you're out there looking for the experience, the opportunity will present itself. Just consider any income you might be passing up as your investment in your own education, as tuition.

Remember Chris Gardner in *The Pursuit of Happyness*? He chose to take an upaid internship with Dean Witter, when he was homeless. What was he, crazy? No. He knew exactly what he was doing. He was investing in the bank of experience, and I believe after six months of that, with his attitude, even if he hadn't become the top intern in his class and gotten hired, he would have taken the knowledge and experience he gained and *still* become incredibly successful, with his own multimillion-dollar brokerage house. Like the old *Rocky* theme song says, he had the "eye of the tiger."

Experience is *not* that hard to come by if we stop thinking we've got to get hired by some company somewhere to get it. Get this in your head big time. Because once you do, you'll find the experience you need to succeed.

Excuse Number Six: I Don't Have a Car

You won't get any sympathy here. Don't forget, when I started my first two businesses, I was too young to drive. My only mode of transportation was a bicycle, my feet, the bus, or my parents. I was reminded of this on a recent business trip to Belize, a poor country in the Western Caribbean. Our tour guide commented that most Belizeans used BMWs. There was a long pause as we looked around. Belize is one of the poorest countries in this half of the world. Then she laughed and added that in Belize, BMW means *"Better Me Walking."*

I'm not going to spend a lot of time on this excuse, because it's really a nonissue. I know, if you don't have wheels, it's a biggie to you. But get real. Remember a few pages back I described a whole business that requires no transportation whatsoever: selling on eBay. Remember Kyle McDonald? He got into an actual house of his own, with a business he ran from his apartment. In any regular eBay type of business, you can order shipping tubes for free from the post office, print your own labels and postage right from home, and do all of your dealings by e-mail and phone. And I showed you other businesses that don't require a car, or even a computer.

Get Up Offa That Thang

You can build all kinds of other businesses from your living room, not just those that can be done on the Internet. There's this 14-year-old girl I'll call Jamie, tutoring kids in math. She's 14, not even a straight-A student, and some of her students are 17 or 18. Their parents bring them to her, and pay her $10 an hour to school their kids! Who says you need wheels to make it?

Remember Oseola McCarty, the washwoman who left all that money for scholarships? She never owned a car in her life. You know, if you had saved up that much money working from home, and really needed a car to accomplish your bigger goals, I think you might have had enough to buy one . . . what do you think?

For businesses that do require you to get out and go places, there are always buses, cabs, and subways to get you where you want to go, just build the costs into your business plan. Build your costs into whatever you charge your customers, just like every other business. It's just the cost of sales. You may even find that using public transportation is a lot cheaper than owning a car, what with $3-a-gallon gas, high insurance rates, repair costs, maintenance costs, and everything else. In major cities, it's also a lot faster and easier to get there if you don't even own a car.

If you're thinking about a retail store, why not open one near enough to your home that you can walk to work or ride a bicycle? Have vendors and associates come to you. The bottom line is this, when you want something badly enough, little things like lack of transportation won't stop you, they'll only slow you down a bit.

Think about it this way: If someone was giving away bags of hundred dollar bills and it required you to travel across town, would you find a way? Of course! When it's important enough, we always find a way. The real question is are your dreams important enough to make them happen, and get rid of all the excuses that are holding you back?

Excuse Number Seven: I'm Just Not Ready

This is sort of the catchall excuse used by people who procrastinate. This excuse is the end of the discussion, the one that covers any and every situation, even when all of our other excuses fail. You've heard it. It doesn't matter what the reasons are, this excuse supersedes everything.

They could have a million bucks in their hand, a paid-for office with a year's free supply of inventory, paid-for advertising, and a payroll backed by a forgivable advance from their bank. They could have a year's paid vacation from their boss so they can get their business started, and they would STILL have a whole list of logical and sensible reasons why they *just aren't quite ready* to get started right now.

It all adds up to time that's being wasted when they could be moving toward a goal of wealth and self-sufficiency. Often, it's because deep down inside they're just afraid. Even though they think they're being smart, they're actually delaying things in every possible way to avoid the risks they perceive. The truth is these procrastinators and perfectionists just don't want it bad enough.

Procrastination

Perhaps you've seen this happen: A bright, energetic man (or woman) has a great idea for a new business. He dreams about leaving the daily grind, the job, and striking out on his own. He studies the market and the more he thinks about it, the more convinced he becomes that this is the big one. The budding businessperson works up a great name for the business, a slogan, and even has a logo created. He even buys some software and writes up a business plan. Talks it up at lunch every day until everyone's tired of hearing about it. But then, nothing happens. Zip.

He never seems to get off the "great idea" stage. When asked, there are plenty of perfectly good, factual reasons why the business never quite gets off the ground. Maybe he's waiting for the market to change, or it changed before he could get in and now he has to wait it out. It never occurs to him to alter his business plan or try a different angle.

Or maybe he just has to save up enough money to start it up, but then his car broke down, you know, and it ate up all the money he'd saved, so he's got to start over. He tried to get a bank loan, but his bank turned him down. And the boss won't give him anymore time off during the day to go to more banks. Lenders, you know, they only work from nine to five. Oh really? Would you stop without pressing for a lunch or Saturday meeting or even a special meeting after work? He'll get there eventually, maybe. He's just not quite ready. Rest assured, when he's really ready he'll go for it.

I suppose the degree of effort and willingness to adapt is directly related to how much you value your dream and how much you're determined to go for it. Some people do manage to break through all this mental clutter and get started. They have the drive and determination, but they're still stuck on planning out every detail perfectly before moving forward. And during, and after. So even when they do get their particular enterprise off the ground, they often discover that all that advance planning and hand wringing was wrong, anyway. Only, they rest their confidence in "The Plan," and tend to miss all the signposts along the way giving them new and different directions to reach their goal.

Be Willing to Change Your Plan to Reach Your Goal

I'm not saying you shouldn't plan and prepare. It's smart to think ahead and know in advance what you're going to do. You just don't want to get so bogged down in your plan that you're spinning your wheels. Young people often succeed simply because they don't know what they're not supposed to be able to do, or what they should be doing according to the so-called smart thinkers. Remember what Colin Powell said, "Don't be afraid to challenge the pros."

Often young people will simply rush headlong into an enterprise or a business. I'm not saying this is how to do it. They won't know exactly how things should be done and they're bound to make many mistakes, but they have lots of energy, tons of creativity, and a clear idea of where they want to end up. When things go wrong, they have the resilience to step back and adapt. To pick themselves up, dust themselves off, and start all over. These are all vital ingredients for success. Of course, if they're smart they'll pick up a mentor along the way to cut out some of the mistakes.

Why Do We Let Excuses Run Our Life?

When speaking I often dissect the "reasons" people give for their failures, so I get asked all the time why people let excuses run their lives. The reason I say for their *failures* is because I haven't found many people who excuse away their own accomplishments, unless they've got a serious self-worth issue going on. There is the common "Just lucky, I guess." brush off, but essentially we enjoy taking the credit and attaboys when we do something good, but we often look to excuse or blame our failures. Why?

Why are people so willing to accept dead-end lives built on dead-end excuses? And why are people so willing to accept that it's just the way things are, that it's us against the world. Like we're the victims. I don't buy that. I've been to Africa on mission trips. I've seen *real* victims.

You Are NOT a Victim

I know the difference between true victims and those people who are bound in fear. You see, the real core behind all of our excuses is fear. Just plain fear. It can be fears of lots of different things, but fear it is nonetheless. Whether people hide behind excuses, do drugs, or lash out at society, fear is at the bottom of it all. We all have fears. What we do with that fear is what determines our destiny.

SECTION III

The Dark Hall of Fear

When you put together all the excuses, all the reasons people give for not going out on their own, for not following their dreams, for not believing in themselves and following their dreams, it really all boils down to one word: *fear.* Fear of the unknown is a common thing and for some people, staying broke or staying in a miserable job or relationship is somehow less uncomfortable than facing the big, bad world and embracing change. Facing the unknown. Facing the "what ifs" of life.

Why do I name fear as the source for all the excuses and other things that hold us back in life? Because we alter our actions based on fear. If a car is hurtling toward you at 100 miles an hour, your heart skips a beat, your breathing kicks into short breaths, and you jump out of the way. You react. We respond to faith, but we *react* to fear. Faith motivates us in a positive way. But it's not our faith that holds us back, it's our fear.

People who are too scared to make a decision, or who procrastinate until they're "ready," are simply reacting differently to their fears. The person who swaggers and threatens you in the mall, and the person who can't look you in the eye when they talk to you, are both reacting to fear. The person full of anger and resentment, and the person overcome by depression . . . all fear. Fear is more than just being scared. I like to spell it out this way:

FEAR: False Expectations that Appear Real

Fear is the opposite of faith, whether faith in God, ourselves, our own abilities and judgment, or in others and other circumstances and opportunities. Fear specializes in falsehood. The operative words are *false* and *appear*. Fear feeds on the worries and doubts that nag us consciously and subconsciously morning, noon, and night, creating *false expectations:* We expect the worst; we expect bad things to happen . . . based on what? Fear is at the heart of most failure, and our fears are what hold us back from the best things in life.

The number one fear is speaking in public—it even tops fear of death. I still remember the first time I faced a big audience. I knew my material backward and forward. I was fully prepared, yet I was trembling like a sixth grader going to his first dance. Come to think of it, I *was* a sixth grader! My first words came out so shaky, I sounded like someone trying to yodel. I think most of my sentences began with "I . . . er . . . um, I mean, uhh . . ." Not to mention my voice was cracking and my throat was dry. What was I so afraid of? We normally think of fear as relating to some imminent physical danger, not just normal life circumstances.

Fear can be a great motivator, although generally hope and a vision or dream is much better and longer lasting. People can do superhuman things out of fear—like the story of the mother who lifted a car off her injured child. Or the night when I was walking home on a dark street and thought someone was following me . . . I never ran so fast in my life. The track coach would have recruited me if he'd seen me sprinting that night!

However, there are some people whose *only* motivator is their fear. They live their lives waiting for it, hiding from it, or being propelled by it. They have to feel threatened to do anything. There are salespeople who start producing only when they fear they're going to be fired, or evicted for nonpayment of rent. In fact, in hardcore sales teams there's a philosophy of "keep 'em hungry." Sometimes that's done by holding out big goals, but I've seen companies bury some poor salesperson in huge financial obligations to keep the burn going.

> We have nothing to fear, but fear itself!
>
> —*Franklin D. Roosevelt*

We Are All Hardwired to Pay Attention to Our Fears

We choose whether we will be controlled by our fears—or control them. I get total silence from audiences whenever I say this, but it's true. Fear of real, physical danger is normal. Even the most experienced soldiers going into battle are afraid. They will tell you that if you don't have fear in that situation, there's something wrong with you. There would be something wrong with me if I told you to live your life without fear. Fear is going to be there whether you like it or not.

Most fear creeps in slowly, stealthily, and builds up in our minds. That is where fear lives, after all, in the mind. It is purely a thought pattern in your brain. And if you can't point to a real danger, like someone having a gun pointed at your head or standing too close to the edge of a cliff, you are afraid of an unknown, of a "maybe." That's a **false expectation.** But the way our mind works, it doesn't know the difference. That unknown something *appears real* to our mind and emotions. In fact, the more we dwell on our fears, the more real they become. Our fears sap our power, our will. We have no way of knowing what might happen or even how it could happen, but we are still afraid of it.

If someone is fearful enough, they will develop elaborate avoidance behaviors. Just like the claustrophobic person, who fears small spaces and crowds, always seems to use the stairs instead of the elevator "for his health." If you fear failure or success, you may become frozen, unwilling to move forward or backward for fear it will come true.

To Fear or Not to Fear, That Is the Choice We Make

The good news, even though you may not have ever considered it—or can even believe it right now—is that **we *choose* to have fear in our lives. Or not to.** We can't eliminate fear, but we *can* choose to control it and not live our lives bound up by it. We can learn to recognize it, call it what it is, and deal with it. That is our choice, as well. As with any emotional issue, the first step is to recognize how fear is at work in our lives and understand the ways it controls us.

There are forces that are stronger, more powerful, and more positive than fear. One of these is faith. I am here to tell you that faith will overcome fear like light overcomes darkness.

Be Not Afraid

When it comes to isolating and controlling the fears that hold you back from success, nothing, I repeat, nothing is stronger than faith.

There is the faith we have in a Higher Power and there is the faith we have in ourselves. Both are powerful forces in the battle against your fears. If you believe in a Higher Power, in God, and I hope you do, you can lean on that faith. You can let it surround you and give you comfort and peace.

Then there is faith in yourself, which is often seen as *self-confidence*. Having faith in yourself will balance and outweigh those deadly doubts and misgivings. Self-faith or self-confidence starts with a conscious choice, a commitment that you make to yourself. Sometimes, it may not feel as real as the fears you wrestle with daily. Until it feels right, you may have to find a way to remind yourself at regular intervals of your abilities and the power you have in your life. You may even have to "fake it until you make it!"

The Magic Bullet: Self-Confidence

The one thing that practically all successful people have in common is an empowering belief in themselves. It may not be a conscious belief; they just know how much they can really do. They know it the same way you know you can breathe and blink your eyes. They don't have to think about, it just is. To me, self-confidence is the magic bullet that can shoot through a million problems and find its way to success.

> *Given equal amounts of intelligence and resources,*
> *a man or woman with positive self-confidence*
> *will almost always accomplish more than*
> *someone without self-confidence.*

That's a pretty powerful statement when you think about it. If you have a level playing field, with everything else being equal—money, looks, education, opportunities . . . every disadvantage, disability, fear, race, or gender issue, you name it—the person with a positive state of mind will almost always come out ahead of the competition. The reason is simple:

> *With self-confidence, your mind will lead you*
> *toward realizing your goals. Wherever your mind*
> *leads you, your body will follow.*

In other words, if your mind *believes* that success is a done deal, your body—the rest of you—will work to fall in line and fulfill that image. Notice I used the word *believe*. I didn't say "if your mind *thinks*" because that's not the same thing. It comes down to the difference between "I think" it's going to happen and *"I know"* it's going to happen.

How Can You Know? How Can You Be Sure?

Super-successful people will tell you that the real state of their mind, when thinking about their objective or goal, is usually, "It's already happened." In other words, they think about their goal the way they would think about it if it were already a historical fact. For them, it *is* a fact.

Olympic athletes see themselves winning, count their strides around the course, see the medal being placed around them, hear the crowd's roar, and watch the band strike up the "Star Spangled Banner."

Top NBA players see the three-pointer slip through the hoop without touching the rim . . . before they shoot. Running ends mentally see themselves slipping through defense, ducking and diving, and crossing the line: touchdown!

Tiger Woods visualizes every hole, all the obstacles, all the yards, and where the sand traps or roughs lie. When he steps out to drive his first ball, he mentally sees it going right to the hole . . . he *knows* where it will go before he swings.

I saw my video game, complete and being enthusiastically played by lots and lots of kids. I saw thousands of teenagers and college students signing up on GoFerretGo and thousands of job offers being placed there by employers. I saw City Capital as a thriving, multimillion-dollar international business . . . long before any of these events actually took place.

Like the Sun Rising in the Morning

Some people are born with self-confidence. Others have developed it because they've been around supportive people all their lives or had mentors who understood these principles and taught them. They have been told repeatedly that they are truly exceptional, that they can make it, that they can do whatever they dream of and passionately seek. So, even thought their goal may be nothing more than a distant dream right now, they still believe in it. It's like it already happened in their minds. I believed. More often than not, this one simple change in perception is the spark that turns it all into reality.

Unfortunately, self-confidence is not something you can just go out and get. It's more like building a muscle. You can't buy a muscular physique. It takes a lot of work. In the same way, you have to work your "confidence" muscle. The only way for most of us to grow our self-confidence is the way an athlete builds up muscles and stamina, skill and precision.

We do this by pushing ourselves out of our Comfort Zones, experiencing little successes along the way, and getting into a habit of success. If you've grown up having a lot of self-doubts or not having the kind of positive encouragement and support I describe, then having this kind of self-confidence may seem like an unreachable goal—like the fabled Holy Grail, intensely desired yet seemingly unattainable. Like something some other people have, but you don't. It doesn't have to be that way.

Self-Confidence and Its Twin: Self-Respect

An important part of the equation is our own self-respect. If we don't respect ourselves, it's hard to trust ourselves, to be confident in who we are and our abilities. It's easy to tell when someone lacks self-respect. No matter how puffed up and confident he appears, he doesn't treat others around him with respect.

If You're Disrespectful to Others, You Cannot Respect Yourself

Self-confidence is where real self-respect starts, too. When we're disrespectful to others, it feeds right back into our feelings about ourselves. Treating others with respect will totally change your whole perception of things because others will start reflecting it back and respecting you, encouraging you and your dreams.

Self-respect is an absolutely necessary ingredient of self-confidence The first person who has to understand and accept this is you. Our culture seems to encourage rudeness and disrespect, and behind all of that are millions of hurting people who have low or no self-respect—no respect for themselves, no self-esteem. And that person will stay at the bottom, always being a hater. But the one he or she is hating the most is him- or herself. If this is you, give it up.

The people we want to be around the most aren't the ones tearing us or others down, it's the ones who lift us up. The ones who have that positive attitude of hope and belief, not the ones who take all the hope out of every situation with their negative attitudes and outlook. The ones who help us believe, who make us want to believe, even when we don't. Be a giver, not a taker. Walk in love and give. Live your life based on abundance at whatever level you are right now, instead of lack. Live based on all that water *in* your glass, not measuring your life by how much water it will take to fill the glass.

Can you get self-confidence in yourself, if you don't have any? Absolutely! Develop your skills. Practice, practice, practice, then practice some more. When you're done, practice some more.

Think about something you are confident about right now and how it got that way. Anything. How about how you sign your name? You don't even think about it, do you? You never worry about whether you can sign your name—you just do it. You've heard your name and known it since before you could even talk, so your comfort with your name is absolute. You could sign it with your eyes closed.

Riding a bike is the same kind of thing. Most of us learn to do that at some time or another. It's something we struggle with, usually with a lot of scrapes and falls along the way. But how do we learn to balance and pedal and turn the handlebars all at the same time?

We practice, fall, get up, practice some more, improve our skills, and perfect them over time. If you're like most people, you've done it so much now that you have total confidence that you can do it again any time you want to. It may have been years since you rode a bicycle, but you know you can. You might be a little wobbly at first, but you have no doubt you can still ride a two-wheeler. It's such a universal truth that people use it as an example, "It's just like riding a bike: once you learn how, you never forget!"

If you think back, you *wanted* to learn how to ride that bike. You saw other kids, maybe your older brother or sister, riding and it represented a kind of freedom. You knew if they could do it, it couldn't be too hard. You could mentally see yourself gliding along, not having to walk every time you wanted to go somewhere. Maybe you could get a paper route or find some kind of job a kid could do once you learned how to ride. You saw yourself achieving all this. You knew it was yours like it had already happened. The learning part was just a little thing between you and the goal you already knew was yours.

As you start to take the necessary steps, with that kind of confidence—that your goal *already belongs to you*—you'll find ways you never thought of to achieve it. You'll meet people who will help you get there. Doesn't matter what it is or how big it is. You'll find a way as long as you keep on keeping on because you'll know you *can* . . . you'll see that goal as real as if you have already achieved it. This attitude is absolutely essential to a happy and successful life. You only get one shot at life . . . there are no dress rehearsals! You've got to believe in yourself, in your dreams, and in the reality of your goals. Throw away those old excuses and fears. They won't help you succeed; they'll only keep you down. You don't need them. If you don't deal with them now, they'll kick in and consume you just when you're on the edge of success.

What's the Alternative?

Let's take a moment to look at the only other option to achieving this level of confidence: **lack of confidence.** Insecurity and self-doubt are two of the greatest deal-killers and success-killers of all. Lack of confidence in our selves, in our dreams and goals, can keep us from even trying. Lack of confidence creates most of the personal misery in relationships as well as in business. The fear that chokes us when we think of moving outside of our Comfort Zone, of confronting issues and people, of dealing with things openly in a relationship, will choke our joy and success in life.

These insecurities and self-doubts get activated real easily. Little things that mean nothing can start arguments and misunderstandings, ruin relationships and careers, and spoil business partnerships. These are the same things that start wars, when perceived insults and long-standing hurts boil over, and people start shooting at each other. These emotions and attitudes can dominate our lives if we let them.

Lack of confidence in ourselves means we don't trust ourselves . . . we don't trust our decisions or our judgment. What a terrible place to be, yet most Americans suffer from this horribly. Most of us aren't born with total confidence in our own abilities and have an underlying fear that if we make a mistake, it'll be a *big* one. That somehow our life's savings may be wiped out in a single act of bad judgment. That if we say "I do" the person will turn into a witch or werewolf overnight. Most folks just aren't naturally comfortable making major decisions, especially where money or relationships are involved and the risk of failure is real.

The good news is we really can build our confidence level if we are willing to step out of our Comfort Zones and push our personal envelopes. The great leap in the process is learning to step out in faith and take whatever actions need to be done to prepare yourself to achieve your goals. In other words, if you want success, do your homework, read the books, get the training, practice, experience, research, dress the part, find mentors, or whatever else you need to do. Having faith in yourself is a lot easier when you know you're prepared for just about anything they can throw at you.

When I had to give that first speech in sixth grade, I was definitely afraid. So to offset that, I got myself mentally well prepared. I'm not talking about using over-preparation to put off the job. I just got serious about what I had to do. I practiced my speech over and over, tweaked my notes, worked my imaginary room. I even gave the speech to a couple of friends to get their feedback on how it sounded.

When I stepped up to that podium, sure, I was shaking like a leaf. But by the time I'd finished my introduction, I was in control. From then on, it became easier and easier. The preparation I had done allowed me to have some small level of confidence that I would do an okay job. That was all I needed, just that little reassurance.

That same scared kid learned to overcome those fears and anxieties and went on to win Future Business Leaders of America's National Title in Speaking and Entrepreneurship in 1999. I learned techniques I still use today to overcome my jitters and fears, and it's allowed me to make presentations in Wall Street boardrooms, to major banks and national corporations, and to thousands and thousands of people around the country.

> People pay for what they do, and still more for what they have allowed themselves to become. And they pay for it very simply; by the lives they lead.
>
> —*James Baldwin*

It's true. There is always a price to pay to face our fear and overcome it, but the alternative is to cower every time we encounter it and to be dominated by the fears that hold us back. We don't always get to set the price we'd *like* to pay, but we always have the choice of giving up and paying the price of failure or paying the price to succeed. How much is this *price*? It's whatever it costs us to have the life we want and achieve our dreams and goals. *How much are you worth?*

Here's something that might help make tackling your fears a little easier. Almost all of our fears fall into two basic areas. Someone's going to write me that they have one that's different, that I don't understand that their fear is too big, but *all* fears are under your ultimate control. It doesn't mean it's easy, but if it were easy everyone would be doing it and we'd all be super successful. This isn't meant to be a scientific, psychological treatise on every category and type of fear. But simplifying them somehow makes my own fears feel smaller and less threatening.

Two Kinds of Fear

Most of the fears that I see immobilizing people boil down to two primary issues: **Fear of People** and **Fear of Failure.** Sometimes I call them FOP and FOF when I speak before a group. That takes the edge off a bit, but these two are nothing to laugh at. They're success killers and create lives of misery.

Fear of People

I regularly speak in front of investor organizations, college business schools, and other professional groups around the country. You'd be amazed at the number of well-educated, otherwise successful people who come up to me afterwards and tell me they would absolutely freeze if they had to stand and talk in front of people. Board meetings give them the shakes; being asked to pray over the Men's Breakfast terrifies them; and even giving a wedding toast is more than they can handle.

> I don't know the key to success, but the key to failure is trying to please everybody.
>
> —*Bill Cosby*

People pleasing can be one way that we compensate for this form of fear. Are you a people pleaser? I see people all the time who try to bend over backward to please their spouse, their boss, their coworkers. They get their lives all twisted up like a pretzel, worrying (there's that false expectation) about offending someone or being rejected. I believe more people avoid pursuing what could be a lucrative sales career because of this one fear over any other reason.

We may think of Fear of People as a fear of messing up, being embarrassed in front of others, having to explain ourselves, stuttering, going mentally blank, or appearing foolish and losing face. Fear of emotional pain. Fear of being judged by what other people *think*, and what they may say about us. Fear of feeling *less than* others.

Fear of People and their rejection of us can keep us from doing the things we want, from expressing our true feelings, and from intimacy in our relationships. How does this fear poison relationships? It keeps two people from being straight and honest with each other. Instead, mind games and word games take the place of honesty. We dance around the issues instead of dealing with them, for fear of insulting our partner.

Fear of People can keep us from standing up in a negotiation, wanting to be everyone's friend and not bruise anyone's feelings. We'll take a smaller piece of the pie if it means keeping the peace. Of course, later on we feel like we've been taken advantage of, and that just reinforces our resentment, lowers our self-esteem, and builds a new level of excuses for later on.

The Walls We Build Keep Us from the Life We Want

We start building these crazy walls to protect ourselves, and in doing so we build walls that keep us back and hold us in. These fences are our own . . . nobody else is holding the key to the gate. But the key is in our own hands: Don't worry about what other people think.

> Don't be afraid to challenge the pros, even in their own backyard.
>
> —*Colin Powell*

When we get all tied up in what other people think, we start to second-guess our own thoughts and dreams.

Like any other fear, Fear of People can hold us back or propel us forward (as we recognize it and determine not to let it rule our life). Don't worry, when you are super successful, all the "I told you so" folks will claim that they saw your potential all along. Heck, some of them will even claim that they were the force behind you going forward.

The Fear of People and what people think or feel is very closely linked to the Fear of Failure.

Fear of Failure

It's important to distinguish the difference between Fear of Failure and our basic desire for self-preservation. One is simple fear, the other is wisdom. The wisdom of self-preservation keeps us from jumping off our roof or crossing a busy street on a green light. Our preference for life is what makes the cancer patient fight to be a cancer survivor. They struggle every day with real fear of losing. And losing means the game's over. You're dead. But some of these terminal patients make the choice to take on the battle anyway. And that change in attitude is often the only reason the doctors can give for why they survive. Self-preservation is good. Wisdom is good.

> There is nothing more tragic than to find an individual bogged down in the length of life, devoid of breadth.
>
> —*Martin Luther King Jr.*

But Fear of Failure breeds procrastination and self-doubt. We wrestle with the unending "what ifs" of life, so afraid of risking failure that we never give success a chance. We fear being alone, being abandoned. We imagine false expectations of what might happen if we venture out into the unknown. If we go for our goals, go for our dreams, what then? Fear of Failure immobilizes us and keeps us from even trying, because "what if I lose?"

In the business world, one of the most crippling of all fears is Fear of Failure. It can plunge us into bad decisions and cause us to pass up golden opportunities. I have seen more businesspeople stall out before they get started, all because of that one fear: *failure*. It is so insidious and so subtle that hardly anyone recognizes it. But for many people, even some of the smartest and most capable people I've known, Fear of Failure is the one roadblock to success they just couldn't seem to overcome.

What's so Bad about Failing, Anyway?

Unless you are choosing to live a mediocre life and remain a failure, failing itself isn't anything to be afraid of, or ashamed of. Success without failure is an impossibility: nobody wins at everything and never loses. Even the Apostles had many shortcomings and failures. One of the greatest politicians and heroes of America was considered by most people to be a dismal failure. I mean, would you vote for someone with this record?

- Failed in business by age 32.
- Ran for the State Legislature and lost at age 33.
- Second failure in business at 34.
- Suffered a nervous breakdown at 37.
- Defeated for Speaker at 39.
- Defeated for Elector at age 41.

Doesn't look so good, does it? This guy couldn't win Dog-catcher! I mean, an Elector is just the person that gets *sent* to the Convention to cast the vote for the real candidate to win the election. What a loser! But he didn't quit. He believed in himself and learned from every failure along the way:

- Ran for Congress—and lost—when he was 44.
- Defeated—again—for Congress at 49.
- Tried running for senator when he was 56—defeated.
- Ran as vice presidential candidate at 57—and lost.
- Went for the Senate again, and lost again. By now he's 59—

Honestly, would *you* have kept on trying this hard, after beating your head against wall after wall for almost 30 years? I have to hand it to him, he kept on trying different positions and campaigns, and didn't give up. Knowing this candidate's lousy record, would you have voted for him for president?

It wasn't until after this string of almost 30 years of failure after failure, that this man—Abraham Lincoln—was elected president in 1860. What if he had quit trying after that last Senate race? What if he had just given up and hung his head in shame after his nervous breakdown? Gone back to some miserable little legal practice and done a little farming on the side? "Old Honest Abe, he's a good lawyer to have if someone steals your cow!" He had every reason to throw in the towel many times over. Who needs that kind of grief? You tried, Abe. Nobody can deny that. But you failed. Give up and live with it.

Would you have even known his name? Would our country still be split down the middle if Lincoln had given up, or let fear of *one more failure* immobilize him? It was Lincoln who turned an unpopular war into the great moral event of our nation's history. And it was unpopular. There was a lot of pressure on Lincoln to let the Confederate States go their own way. After all, the North had all the industry, and who cared about all those slaves?—They were just personal property anyway. A lot of people weren't comfortable with slavery, but many more felt like someone else's property was none of their business.

How many millions of people would have stayed in chains for months and years longer because some other leader might have given in? Taken the easy route? What would some other leader who hadn't gone through as much misery, loss, and *failure* as Honest Abe have done? Slavery couldn't last forever, but how much longer might it have hung on? How many more lives would have been torn apart and enslaved with no hope?

Because Lincoln didn't quit and wouldn't give up, there was emancipation. It was because of his own failures that he had the resolve to stick it out.

In some of the darkest, most hopeless days of World War II, when it looked like Hitler could not be stopped, Winston Churchill gave a speech to Harrow, his old school. It was the thick of the Blitz,

1941, the Battle of London, with nightly bombing raids, and England felt very much alone—and scared. America was still officially neutral. That year the great British statesman, pausing to look around at his audience and to add emphasis to each word, said:

> *Never give in.*
> *Never,*
> *Never,*
> *Never,*
> *NEVER!*
> *In nothing great or small,*
> *Large or petty,*
> *Never give in except to convictions of honour and good sense.*
> *Never yield to force,*
> *Never yield to the apparently overwhelming might of the enemy.*

Many times the best winning strategy is to just be determined to win. Don't take no for an answer. I've seen my share of football games where the team that won't quit, that plays down to the last second, gets the goal that takes the championship. Remember the story of David and his brothers? He didn't listen to them when they cut him down. What did he do? He "turned from them to another." David didn't care what they thought; he was focused on success. David wouldn't allow anyone to keep him from his goal.

> Success is not final, failure is not fatal: it is the courage to continue that counts.
>
> —*Winston Churchill*

What *is* failure, anyway? When a boxer gets knocked down to the mat, is he some loser? Not! The boxer who gets knocked down isn't a loser . . . *unless he stays beat down, and doesn't get back up.* That's the secret: Get back up when you've been knocked down. Just get back up, one more time—*and don't quit!*

Defeat is simply a signal to press onward.

—*Helen Keller*

Helen Keller should know about getting back up. She was born blind and deaf, and people assumed she couldn't speak either. She was a wild child, but her mentor Annie Sullivan helped her navigate all these obstacles and find her voice, and she became known all over the world, inspiring people to overcome their fears and excuses and go for it.

Fear of Failure Mixes It Up with Fear of People

Our fears don't operate in some vacuum. They tangle and wrangle and mix together, making all sorts of vicious, poisonous cocktails of fear. We fear more than just losing our shirt; we fear having other people we respect *see* us lose our shirt. It's the fear of being the greater fool, the one who buys the house just as the market crashes or just before being laid off. Embarrassment over failure isn't easy to overcome, because our failures tend to be noticed and commented on by concerned family and friends, as well as those other people in our life we wish would just go away.

Our fears and actual reality may or may not be connected. Usually, it's more like the old adage about how we see a glass of water: Is the glass half empty, or is it half full? Technically, both of the statements are true, but our personal viewpoint filters the results. **The difference is in how we look at the glass.** Our viewpoint, our perception, is a reflection of our attitude toward life.

Your Perceptions Become Your Reality

If we see every glass as half empty all the time, then all we see is what we lack. We feel *less than adequate*. We fear losing what little we have.

We can choose to change our outlook to one of success. This isn't some "don't worry, be happy" mush. We can choose to see the positive in life instead of all the negatives and "why it *won't* work" excuses.

Our glass—our life—is half full. We have abundance, we are enough, we are okay. It's true: *perception is reality*. So change your perception, and you change your reality. Some see failure as being defeated, but others see it as a chance to start over on a new leaf. The only difference is in our mind, and *the seat of all fear is in our mind, not in things that are real.*

Do You Play to Win, or Play Not to Lose?

The clear extension of our perception is seen in how we take on life. If we only focus on what we lack, we feel weak and hold back, afraid of losing. When we see abundance, we feel empowered and act boldly.

> I do not think there is any other quality so essential to success of any kind as the quality of perseverance. It overcomes almost everything, even nature.
>
> —*John D. Rockefeller*

In team sports, the defensive team plays not to lose, to hold ground, and to defend the castle. If that was the entire team strategy, there would never be a score. The city under siege is always at the mercy of the unlimited resources of the offensive army. *We can't win defensive battles,* whether on the field, on the chessboard, on the battleground, or in our lives. While a strong defense will hold down the other team's ability to score, and will occasionally intercept and score some points themselves, you can have the very best defense in the NFL and lose every game. Why? Because you can't win a defensive battle, **it takes offense to win.**

The primary purpose of defense is only to block the other team, not to offensively go forward and make plays to win. In our lives, we must play to *win. But to do this, we must have hope that we will gain something in the process.*

Fear of Loss versus Hope of Gain

We've already covered Fear of Failure as one of our fears, and Fear of Loss is really a component of this. But here I'm talking more about the motivators and attitudes that govern our decision making.

The person who always sees the half-empty glass makes decisions based on perceptions of what they lack; they fear losing what little they have.

For example, some feel an inner pressure to invest in some project, business, or stock *to avoid losing out* on the deal of the century. Or they stay in a bad relationship way too long . . . avoiding the loss of companionship. Some people pull out investments when the market is down, afraid they could be the last one standing when the music stops. These are classic examples of basing our actions on Fear of Loss, and both involve a significant amount of gnawing and gnashing of teeth.

Yet Hope of Gain is the motivator that looks at the opportunity and analyzes the chances of making a good return on investment, then takes positive, decisive action. Once our decision is made, there is very little worrying and fretting because we haven't bet the farm, and we haven't acted because of fear.

Not Making a Decision Is Making a Decision

On the other hand, *not* taking positive action is the only sure way to lose, and every day lost costs us more (this is the dark side of the Time Value of Money). The first step is to have the *confidence to decide* to decide. Even just to make the decision that you will *not let indecision become your default*, ever again. Make positive decisions in the direction of achieving your dreams and goal, not entrenched, negative decisions because you're afraid of what *might* happen.

Once we make that positive decision, it's not always easy. But the decision to move on our dreams and goals is the key that unlocks the door. Once we open that door of possibilities, it's up to us to keep the faith—to not give up, to be persistent and insistent that success will be ours. Look how President Calvin Coolidge summed up the importance of persistence versus all the excuses that people let run (and ruin) their lives:

> *Nothing in this world can take the place of persistence. Talent will not; nothing is more common than unsuccessful people with talent. Genius will not; unrewarded genius is almost a proverb. Education will not; the world is full of educated derelicts. Persistence and determination alone are omnipotent. The slogan "press on" has solved and always will solve the problems of the human race.*

Dad put it another way. He always recited this little poem my grandfather told him:

> *If a task has once begun.*
> *Never leave it til it's done.*
> *Be the labor great or small.*
> *Do it well or not at all.*

In other words, stick to your guns. Be persistent and don't let other people talk you out of your goals and dreams. Make your decisions based on hope and faith, not fear.

Choosing Failure; Choosing Success

When I talk about excuses and fear, I'm not trying to blame or put anybody down. We all have our own things to deal with, and each of us sees different aspects of ourselves within the sections of this book. If we asked someone close to us to read this book and tell us what *they* see in *our* lives, it might be surprising. In fact, I encourage you to do that. Sometimes the things we think we're really good at hiding from others, are right out there in the open, all the time. Like the drunk who thinks he's real smooth and cool . . . although everyone knows he's hammered. We figure what goes on in our head stays in our head, but it isn't so.

People around us see more than we think they do. We can spend our whole lives wearing masks and pretending everything is okay, that we're cool or tough or whatever, but those around us know. We can spend our whole lives building walls to protect us so we never get hurt, but in the end, like campers in the middle of a protective ring of fire, with wolves circling around them, we become prisoners of our own walls. The wolves are all in our head, already in charge, dominating our thoughts and actions and filling us with fear.

Recognize Yourself?

We have all wrestled with the Fear of People or Fear of Failure in some area of our lives. Even great heroes honestly admit that courage isn't the absence of fear, but the overcoming of fear. Great men and women have always had to overcome the same fears and doubts that plague you, me, and all of us. Fear of People and Fear of Failure are two of the greatest enemies of success.

Likewise, everybody makes excuses once in awhile. It's natural. But some people become real pros at bouncing blame back onto everyone else. If some of the excuses we talked about are your automatic answers to every situation, your "go to" script, you may be guilty of imprisoning yourself in the role of the victim. Even if you only say these things to yourself, you may be playing the blame game.

Choice is a central theme in the scriptures, and it is the key to everything good—and bad—in our lives. Choice can mean taking responsibility and taking positive, forward-moving actions and decisions to win. It can also mean:

- Defaulting to negative, sit-and-hold strategies and making decisions *not to lose*, rather than taking actions *to win*.

- Deciding to be indecisive because indecisiveness is itself a decision. When we are indecisive, we are really making a decision to let circumstances happen to us. With indecision, we are *deciding* to yield our destiny and any control we may have to other people or circumstances. Ultimately, we are deciding to be a victim of "I shoulda," "I coulda," and "If I'd only."

We have the innate ability to make a choice inside our head; "Am I going to settle for less and just be comfortable where I am, or am I going to take advantage of every opportunity before me and actually *make* something of my life?" Are you *worth* it? I think you are, but do *you? Really?*

> There are some people that if they don't know, you can't tell them.
>
> —*Louis Armstrong*

Each of us consciously makes these choices hundreds of times each day. You can lead people to water but you can't make them drink. Shoot, you could tie them up, put concrete on their boots, and throw them in the water, but they *still* won't drink the water. You can strap them down and turn on a fire hose to make them drink, and they won't drink until they're ready. We make conscious choices in our lives, based on our perceptions, based on our fears, and based on our pattern of excuses. Or based on our faith and hope and belief that we will achieve our goals, without allowing ourselves excuses.

Most People *Choose* to Be Failures

I know many people will never agree with this, but I consider it to be an absolute. I've seen people react and leave the auditorium ticked off, right in the middle of my talk. I feel sorry for them, but it doesn't matter; it's their choice. Don't write me about this, okay? It's true in your life and mine, whether we like it or not. We either choose to be successful or we choose *not* to be successful. This *can* be a choice by default . . . if we don't consciously choose either, we fail.

It's not about whether we raise our hand or not, or say, *"Hey! I want be a success!"* We live our vote by our actions everyday. I know many people want to lose weight. Heck, I want to lose weight too, but are my actions saying that I want to lose weight? No. Am I going out and exercising? No.

I'm not discounting the need to lose weight. There's a real epidemic of obesity in our country, especially among kids, fueled by fast food and unhealthy, high-calorie, high-fat foods that taste ohhh-so-good.

I can come up with a million excuses why I can't lose weight. "I'm a busy executive. I run a company. I'm just stress eating. I'll do it after . . . whatever." Does anyone believe any of my junk except me? No! They see all the junk piling up in my trunk.

I manage to take on new challenges every day. I put whatever focus is necessary on the things that are important to me. I make time for everything else. I can always figure out a way to set aside hours to play video games when I want to.

So, if I *really* wanted to lose the weight, if it was important to me, I could find a way, period. But *I choose not to* and my results speak for themselves. But you see my real intention when I choose to have that extra piece of fried lobster and the key lime pie. It's the same with success and every other decision in life. You can choose it or not, regardless of your circumstances. If you think you can, or if you think you can't, you're right . . . either way.

Napoleon Hill summed it up best when he said, "Whatever the mind of man can conceive and believe in, it will achieve." And that includes believing in your own success—*or* believing in all the excuses for mediocrity and failure. You make the terms and conditions that you live your life by. You make the decision. You make the deal. What kind of bargain do you want?

Life

I bargained with Life for a penny,
And Life would pay no more,
However I begged at evening

When I counted my scanty store.
For Life is a just employer,
He gives you what you ask,
But once you have set the wages,
Why, you must bear the task.
I worked for a menial's hire,
Only to learn, dismayed,
That any wage I had asked of Life,
Life would have willingly paid.

—Unknown

What makes the difference? It's all in the perceptions, the decisions, the choices, and the bargains we make in our life.

Many of City Capital's private investors have been medical professionals. You wouldn't believe how many doctors have told me stories of having two terminal patients literally side by side in the hospital, or being treated with the same treatment in their practice. One patient doesn't recover or seems to get worse, while the other recovers completely. I talked about this in the section on fear. The doctors often have no medical reason why one patient should live and one shouldn't except that one said, "I'm not going to let it beat me." The one thing that keeps them alive while the patient in the bed next to her dies is her attitude and perception. The doctor can only shake her head. It wasn't the brilliance of the treatment; it was the mindset of the patient.

Thou art snared with the words of thy mouth, thou art taken with the words of thy mouth.

—*Proverbs 6:2*

This is just as true for people with colds, flu, you name it. We all know the person who catches everything that comes around. We also know the ones who have never been sick a day in their life. Proverbs is saying basically we're "hung by our tongue" when we talk like this and believe ourselves.

Some people live life in a full, positive way. They walk through life with the mindset that they can and will overcome whatever obstacles come up to stop them. Others just don't. That's all. They just live defeated lives. Have you ever heard the expression "He died of a broken heart?" Huh? How can someone die of a broken heart? You can actually die—with nothing actually wrong with you, not from a heart attack, and not because your heart has anything physically wrong with it at all.

If your will to live is just gone, the body's just going to shut down. Finding the will to live and purpose in life again, like after losing a spouse, can mean finding the way out of the grief and anguish caused by her death. It's all in the mind, in the outlook.

Your Mind Is Very Powerful

The human mind is more powerful than the fastest, biggest supercomputer in the world. In fact, human minds created that computer, and it still has more limitations than a human mind. The supercomputer may be able to process numbers and facts a gazillion times faster, but it doesn't think. It calculates, analyzes, and interprets data, but it can't *think*. In fact, science still can't tell us exactly how we think. How we reason. How our mind—gray matter, flesh and blood and electrical synapses—can do something as simple as, say, remember a face or voice from 10 years ago in a split second? We know we use less than 10 percent of our brainpower, and within that is enough power to heal the body—or shut it down. It's happened before.

The excuses and inner fears that influence how we perceive risk and opportunity and life—ultimately become our reality. They are of our own choosing. We choose to buddy up to them, to embrace them and hold onto them, to be comfortable with these wolves in our lives. Or we can choose to reject them, confront them, and challenge them for control of ourselves and our destiny. We can decide to chart a new course, get ourselves a little uncomfortable, and achieve our dream.

The alternative to a life of success, of overcoming our fears and excuses, is a life of misery and mediocrity, bound up in the fears and excuses that we create. This is the life of a victim, moved and controlled by outside forces his or her entire life.

The alternative to being a victim is to be proactive and to take responsibility for your actions. Instead of constantly blaming others, take stock and think how *you* could have contributed to the situation, and how you can change things in the future. Ask yourself, "Was I at fault?" or "Was it really just bad luck/good luck/someone else that caused my problem?" These are tough questions and they require serious self-assessment. Honest answers will get you out of a rut that you shouldn't be in.

I believe that a life as an overcomer is much richer than life as a victim. I hope you choose to live a limitless life. And it *really is* your choice.

SECTION IV

Empowerment versus Victimhood

Sooner or later people caught up in excuses and blame tend to develop a *victim mentality*. I have known too many people in my life who were terminal victims. "Professional Victims," I call them. I'm not making light of their suffering. Their excuse may be childhood abuse, or losing their job, or discrimination, or a boss or spouse who took them for granted. It's not whether they were actually "done wrong" that matters. What matters is what they *do* with their life in the face of all their injury and hurt.

I'm not talking about people who occasionally make up some lie about why they are late for work. I'm talking about those who freely blame everyone and everything around them as their excuse for failure. They aren't making up a lie, at least not in their minds. They *actually believe* that every time something goes wrong in their lives, it is someone else's fault. Or some unknown force like "Lady Luck." In other words, *they are always the victim*. They are usually unhappy because in their minds—actually, even deeper down inside—they are convinced they are powerless to change things in their lives.

"It's Not My Fault"

Do you have a victim mentality? Do you ever feel as if others are victimizing you, or somehow standing in your way? Could you be a Professional Victim? Let's do a little test. How often have you found yourself saying these phrases?

- It's not my fault.
- I'm just unlucky, I guess.
- I never seem to win.
- If only I'd had . . .
- What do you expect?
- I could, if it wasn't for . . .
- He (or she) makes me so mad.

- I can't help it.
- You don't understand . . .

The reality is, every time we make the old victim excuses, we give away our power to other people in our lives. But Professional Victims *like* being a victim.

Huh? How could anyone like being a victim? If you think about it, at least on the surface, being a victim doesn't sound so great. Why would anyone want to feel like they're powerless? Oh, they may not use the term *victim*, but when someone starts their sentences with "I can't . . ." that means *"something else is more powerful than I can control!"* But imagine an ad on Craigslist to become a Professional Victim and consider the benefits:

Ever feel like the world's on your shoulders? Ever feel like you can't go on?

Become a Professional Victim!

It's easy, with the **Professional Victim Home Study Course!**

- Never feel like you have to be responsible for your own life ever again.
- Learn how to find someone or something to blame in as little as 60 seconds, so you'll NEVER be responsible for any failure or shortcomings.
- Regardless of your ethnicity or gender, quickly identify the most likely ones around you who are holding down your real potential.
- How to harness the power of powerful phrases to offset failure like: "If I really wanted to," "You don't understand," and over 100 more, all on an easy-to-use pocket card.

PLUS get . . .

- The **Top 25 Greatest Blame Excuses,** including, "You make me so . . ." and "You hurt me . . ." and many more for every occasion!
- One whole chapter is devoted to the most powerful excuse word of all: **IF**—as used by Master Victims everywhere to create indisputable excuses on the fly.
- How to deflect any focus on shortcomings to others, through blame and faultfinding.
- How to manipulate emotions and run other peoples' lives. (*It's so much easier to run someone else's life than your own!* And you get to be right whether they succeed or fail!)
- Free bonus report: *"I Told You So!"* How and where to use this for maximum effect.
- Special subliminal tapes will reinforce that, no matter what the problem is, it's not your fault. It never was!

Still not sure? Try our 30-day Free Trial. If you're not satisfied, we'll keep your money anyway, to help PROVE to you how easy it is to become a Professional Victim.

I could go on playing with this advertisement, but I think you get the point. Being a Professional Victim is like getting a free pass from personal responsibility. If everything is someone else's fault, then nothing is the person's fault. If everything good that happens is due to outside circumstances, there's no risk in his or her life.

If you try to challenge a person with the victim mentality—like, with a "reality check"—if you question his excuse or his rationale, he probably will react with anger or get defensive. After all, if you only knew how bad he had it, you wouldn't be asking him to justify it. He will present logical and rational-sounding evidence why others are to blame for his lot in life.

Victims don't ever have to examine their own shortcomings. They can totally ignore all the signs that say it's time to change their approach to life and work. However, even though they're unhappy, don't be fooled. This mindset is actually more comfortable to them than the alternative, which is to take responsibility for their own actions.

Responsibility and Power versus Blame and Powerlessness

The Professional Victim is really saying, "Other people or other events derailed my plans, and I'm incapable of overcoming these things. The failures in my life *aren't my fault*." If it's not their fault, then they are not responsible for their own life.

Responsibility is at the bottom of what we're talking about here. Most of us would say we're responsible, but are we? The ultimate responsibility is taking charge of our own life. Other people and other circumstances cannot keep us from our goals, unless we let them. And whenever we try to pass the blame on to some person or circumstance in our life, *we give up our power*. Responsibility is where our true power begins.

> To whom much is given, much will be required.
>
> —*Luke 12:48*

It works both ways: With power also comes responsibility. The two go hand in hand. There are people who don't like that, who are scared to death of taking on more responsibility, even when it means more power in their life. Even when it means more recognition and more wealth. We've talked about the fact that there is a price to pay for success. Part of that price is carrying the responsibility that comes with your success.

Some people don't want to pay this price. They may want what success can bring them, but they want to be able to be irresponsible with it, to do what they want, when they want, with their own selfish self. In fact, for many, their whole definition of success can be summed up this way: "Hey, if you got it, flaunt it. I'm no role model. I have the right to act any way I want."

Everyone already knows you can act any way you want. That's nothing new. Money didn't cause it. Fame didn't cause it. "So why act like a selfish brat, like an idiot, or someone who thinks only of themselves?" No excuse for that either. No growing up in the hood, going a little crazy . . . none of that. It's about who you are as a person. "To whom much is given, much will be required." All the kids that see these fools flying high—driving Hummers and flashing bling—don't have any of "it" to flaunt for themselves (whatever "it" is that they see as making someone successful). They see this fake "superstar" image of success without all the work and responsibility that goes with it, and think that's what it's all about.

Thomas Stanley and William Danko, authors of *The Millionaire Next Door* (New York: Pocket Books, 1996) did a great analysis of exactly what an average millionaire is like, how they dress, what they drive, where they live. What Stanley and Danko found flies in the face of all the media hype and bogus celebrity images.

Most millionaires don't live in mansions, don't wear inexpensive suits, and drive American-made cars. Over half drive Fords! And 36 percent buy used cars rather than new! Eighty percent of American millionaires did not inherit their money, and two-thirds made their millions as self-employed entrepreneurs.

Oh, and about showing off the bling, when it comes to Gucci shoes, Rolex watches, and designer clothes, they're not interested. Half have never spent $235 for a watch or more than $140 on a pair of shoes (forget those Jordans and Nikes!) and less than 25 percent would spend $600 for a suit.

You see, real success isn't about showing off all the status symbols. It's not about trying to impress anyone. Truly successful people don't care if they impress you with their importance or wealth anyway. They care about getting real financial control over their own lives, and that starts with taking responsibility, not flashing the cash.

Power concedes nothing without a demand. It never did and it never will.

—*Frederick Douglass*

We all have responsibilities. You can walk away from yours, but you'll *never* be a success, no matter how much bling you wave in the camera lens. No responsibility means **no real power,** and if you choose to be powerless, to give up your power like that, you don't stand any chance of being truly successful, of having your dreams. You lose, game over. Everything you do and all your accomplishments in the boardroom, in the studio, or on the street mean nothing. If you're not willing to be responsible, you can't be a winner, and all that's left is failure and mediocrity, the same-old, same-old.

> *No responsibility means no control. No control means*
> *no power. No power means no success.*
> *No success = LOSER!*

Look, I know how it is. Being told to "be responsible" is like telling a teenager to stop listening to hip hop music. You might as well yell at a telephone pole. The reality is that **being responsible trains us for success.** Being irresponsible will drag you down. I see so many try to slide by, thinking, "Hey! I'm busy right now having fun in my life. I'll party for a few years and then I'll get serious." This line of thinking just makes it take years longer to reach your dream; years you'll have to keep struggling, trying to keep your head above water, barely making it and wondering why.

Worse, if you aren't responsible for your own life—and I mean managing every little detail—then other people and other things are in control. No responsibility, no control. Responsibility means you're in control. Responsibility means you're empowered for success. So take charge of your own life and get on the path right now that you need to be on to reach your goals.

What about, "If It's God's Will"?

When I'm speaking with congregations about stewardship and money matters, I find so many people who faithfully pray to God to help them, to bring them more money or fix their car, or whatever. Often these same people will dismiss my suggestions about making a budget and sticking to it. Or they'll add, "If it's God's will" to everything they say, like "I'll get my rent money together—*if it's God's will.*"

> People may fail many times, but they become failures only when they begin to blame someone else.
>
> —*Anonymous*

Why do I use this quote when talking about God's will? Because we have to recognize that using God as an excuse is nothing more than a sideways attempt to blame Him for your problems. After all, you *could* have accomplished your goal, but God must have not wanted you to, for whatever lame reason you come up with. Maybe it was to "teach you to be humble," or something equally off base. You really think it was God's will for you to get diabetes? Like He tied you to the table and forced that fork in your mouth. Where's your responsibility in this? He gave you plenty of information and warnings along the way. God isn't in the business of holding you back, keeping you broke, or giving you a disease. He doesn't cause your marriage to break up or you to be laid off from work. Don't blame God.

Here's my point: I believe wholeheartedly in God and his power. However, if you do a half-hearted job and then sit back and say, "I'll succeed here if it is God's will," you are setting up God as the scapegoat for your lack of effort. For instance, if you go to a job interview in shorts and a T-shirt and you're not hired, it's not that God didn't want you to have the job. It's because you didn't do your part to be successful. It was *you*, not God who failed.

We don't just blame God, we blame the people around us. We blame the circumstances of life. We blame anything and everyone—but ourselves. Misfortunes and bad luck can happen to anyone. In fact, they *do* happen to *everyone*.

> The rain falls on the just and the unjust.
>
> —*Matthew 5:45*

You can get speeding tickets, you may even have a car crash. (Who chose how fast to drive?) You may have unscrupulous partners who steal you blind. (Who decided to enter the relationship? Who ignored the necessary oversights and due diligence?) You may lose out in a promotion or have someone you love betray you. The difference between Professional Victims and Winners is not whether they have to deal with the same things, or if they're somehow "lucky." The difference lies in how they deal with these kinds of life circumstances.

Professional Victims will wallow in self-pity and draw out their self-mourning indefinitely. Victims will choose to hold on to their anger and resentment at the rotten individual who betrayed them or caused their misery. The longer they cling to that anger, the deeper into victimhood and powerlessness they sink. Their mindset begins to define who they are.

I see so many people who just seem to waste their whole lives in the Victimhood cycle and create this generational mindset of victims, of being dependent on someone else to get by. This may spill over into being dependent on government programs, of "entitlement," of thinking they're owed something.

What most government entitlement programs really amount to is a handout. Yes, there are government "safety net" programs to help people short-term get out of bad financial situations. There are programs to help those who cannot physically take care of themselves. But there are also healthy, able people who believe the government should take care of them, and they're not willing to go after more than that. How can anyone be satisfied and successful living in a run-down slum house with a broken-down car, just sitting around on his butt waiting for the government check to arrive, if he's able to work and provide for himself and his family? And don't say there aren't any jobs . . . we've already covered loads of ways to make money outside of any job. Any system that encourages this kind of dependent life for people is a system that helps create failure by stripping away personal power and responsibility.

Actually, I've never met anyone in these circumstances who is really happy anyway. Most are mad at the world. But the solution isn't to ask for more handouts, it's to determine within ourselves that we'll break the cycle.

> Don't feel entitled to anything you didn't sweat and struggle for.
>
> —*Marian Wright Edelman*

Don't get me wrong, I support any program to help people in poverty, but the program's objective should be to offer individuals a leg up, a way out of whatever straits they find themselves in, and *not* a handout. People who have bought into a life of entitlement figure the smart money is to stretch out the free checks and food and HUD rent vouchers as long as possible . . . in some cases for generations. The spirit of greatness and success inside is slowly beat out of them, and they willingly become "victims" of society and dependent on a system that destroys any hope.

In my opinion, the African American slaves in our past were freer in their minds than people hooked on most government programs. In fact, *hooked* is an appropriate word to use because they have no more real sense of power in their own minds and lives than someone strung out on drugs. The subtle, and not so subtle, demeaning nature of being totally dependent can drag anyone down.

Culture of Hopelessness

How do you get over this culture of hopelessness and helplessness in our inner cities? Sometimes it seems like an almost impossible situation. There's that whole negative environment that the people are surrounded with day in and day out. Violence. Hopelessness.

Perception really is reality. Somehow we have to break down the mental barriers and expose them to all the other possibilities in their life. If people aren't aware that *the options are all inside themselve*s, how can we ever expect them to dream? Or to believe in and to act on their dreams?

Right now the self-appointed national and local leadership in certain communities aren't very good examples—some are even on the take. Many more are silent about the drugs, violence, and teenage pregnancies that this culture of hopelessness has created. And worse, over the years they've built up organizations that benefit from keeping the poor, poor. They have a vested interest in keeping things the way they are. And people within the communities suffer as a result.

This was the main reason I decided to do a nationwide Urban Wealth Tour, to bring this message to urban youths all across America. The message in this book is the message I'm putting out there, that you have the potential inside you. Don't look at circumstances or other people as your problem. If you want better, go for it. Believe in your dreams and don't listen to the losers who would hold you down, no matter who they are.

Change Your Life, Break the Cycle

Okay, let's clear our minds of all the hopelessness, entitlement, and disempowerment that has dragged down so many of our brothers and sisters. Let's look at what *you* can do to rise above all this in your own life. First, make it a determined goal in your life to break the cycle, to lay down all the excuses, break away from the entitlement programs that enslave people's minds and lives, and get serious about your life and your future.

A real good place to start is in how we look at sex, marriage, and children. I don't really care what all the talking heads on television say, if a girl gets married before having children, there's a greater chance of raising her child in a two-parent home. If a boy and girl make a baby irresponsibly, the odds are stacked against their relationship, their finances, their life . . . and their child. If you really love each other and want a child, wait. People need to get their lives together before they go popping out babies. They must make the decision to marry carefully, prayerfully, and choose not to get pregnant or impregnate anyone else outside of marriage.

I know I'm preaching, but the numbers are staggering. Up to 40 percent of girls age 15 to 19 are having babies—that's 40 out of 100! That adds up to dozens of babies in every high school and thousands more in colleges all over the country—every year. At least that many or more end their pregnancy in abortion—a sad note on our "me" culture and its bitter fruits. And it's even higher among blacks and Latinos in urban communities.

Sex and Business—Your Business

You can be ready to go out and beat the world. But the minute you start making babies, you start down a path that's real, real hard to deal with. It ties you down and keeps you from being free to move and take financial risks. It makes going to night school or college a major undertaking. You have to think first about taking whatever job you can get to support your family and then, maybe, how you can start your business career.

Having babies probably keeps more people from climbing out of poverty than drugs or crime. I'm not saying that babies are a bad thing, but only at the right time—when you're in a strong relationship and ready financially. MeShelle and I have two beautiful children who are a blessing. But if you're still a teenager and not married, having babies is a big, *big* mistake. It can affect every decision you make afterward about business and a career.

Even though I am a Christian and I have strong beliefs, this is not a lecture about morals. I'm going to set aside my Bible and talk to you about the business facts of life. No matter how cute and cuddly babies are, they have to be provided for 24/7/365 for a long, long time. At least as long into the future as you've probably been alive!

How can you commit to do that and do what it takes to become a world-class entrepreneur? It's like trying to run for a touchdown with big concrete blocks chained to your legs.

I'm sure you know someone, somewhere you can point to who made it despite being young, broke, and caring for a child. But I'll bet you know plenty of other friends and relatives, or kids you went to school with, who had to put their entire life on hold because of having a baby. It's a shame because so many of those people are bright, creative people. Like the old Negro College Fund ads used to say, "A mind is a terrible thing to waste."

Having sex is easy. Getting pregnant—or getting some girl pregnant—that part happens in an instant. Fulfilling your responsibility as a parent for the rest of that child's life, *that's hard work!* So if you want to avoid the hard part, *avoid the easy part first*. Get your own life going and growing, get your own head screwed on right so you can honestly take care of yourself, your family, and save money . . . then and only then consider having a child. And if you are going to have a child with somebody, be totally committed to that person and know he or she is totally committed to you. A real good sign of this is that the two of you are married. Another good sign is that the two of you can intelligently discuss and plan for that child in your life before it just "happens." And a real good benchmark is that you two can calmly discuss financial goals and budgets together.

Hey, I'm talking to young men and teens out there who act as if sex is a scavenger hunt—see how many you can rack up. It's no wonder you might think that way, with all the songs about bitches and hos. Rap artists make it sound like girls are just there to give boys pleasure. Get you hot and juiced up. They make girls think that the hotter you look, the more you can get guys worked up. Brother and sister, the truth is life is about so much more than all that. And you have *nothing* if you treat other people like nothing. Who are *you?* Respect others, and you show how much you respect yourself.

But I'm not just talking to the young men, I'm also talking to the young women out there who are living up—or down—to that image. You have a voice in this, too. And being a victim isn't the only voice. Getting pregnant to hook an unsure relationship or "making him pay" isn't the only choice. Saying "No" is another. Saying, "after we're married" is another. This isn't about some popularity contest; this is your life, and the life of your baby.

You can't use excuses and blame to compensate for failure, especially in this most important area. Period. Not if you want to achieve anything in your life. Not if you want your goals and dreams to have a chance. Not if you want your children to have the chance to live out their dreams. Most important, not if you want to live a life of power, instead of victimhood. Change your life and break the cycle once and for all.

Empowerment

Excuses and blame drain away the power in your life. Taking charge of your own life—taking responsibility for your successes or failures—builds your power. Empowerment is an absolutely essential element.

Empowered people make things happen. Disempowered people are helpless and unable to achieve anything. Empowered people change communities, change countries. Weak and beat-down people wait on others to do things, then complain about how messed up things are. Other people and systems and circumstances are to blame for everything in their lives, and they are helpless to change things. Their destiny is in the hands of others. They have no power.

President Harry Truman is famous for having a sign on his desk that read **The Buck Stops Here.** It's a philosophy we can take to heart. The "buck" of personal responsibility for our life stops with us. I have said this before: **If it is to be, it really is up to me.** So instead of taking the easy way out, instead of falling back on blame and resentment, instead of being a victim and "passing the buck," take honest, personal responsibility for your actions. And then take responsibility for your life, right now. When you feel like playing the blame game, look in the mirror and repeat this phrase:

I am the one who controls my life. I am the one who
will make it work. And if it fails, for whatever
reason, I am responsible for that, too. Every reality
in my life is my responsibility. Period.

But what about when other people really do hurt us, and do us wrong? Winners also forgive. They will forgive the person who did them wrong and they will forgive themselves. Sometimes this is the hardest choice to make, but the person who has chosen success—in business or in relationships—knows that forgiveness is the key to open the prison door, to take back your power. When you can honestly forgive, you can let go of the anger that holds you back and infects your daily peace of mind.

Forgiveness Is a Key to Overcoming

Forgiveness doesn't always come easy, but I encourage you to develop a habit pattern of forgiving *and* forgetting, quickly, whenever you perceive any wrong done. Even small affronts and insults, little things at the grocery store and gas station that bug you. Make it a habit, so when the big things come along, you've exercised that "forgiveness muscle" and are able to take on the task. Ultimately, forgiveness is a decision, a mental process that we, and we alone, control. The only person who suffers when we hold onto anger and resentment is *us*.

If you forgive and don't forget about it, you haven't really forgiven. When you *choose* to forgive the jerk who cuts you off in traffic, and just forget about it, neither he nor the circumstance dominates any part of your mind. You made the choice. You no longer feel powerless and angry, but empowered. But when you hold onto the anger and resentment, you are giving up your power because the negative feelings keep going round and round, dominating your thoughts. Forgiveness is *your* choice to make. You're *taking charge* of your life and life circumstances, when you're forgiving.

No, I don't know what you've been through. And even though *you* matter, the circumstances that brought you to this moment are only that: circumstances. None were accidental. Some were good and some were bad.

Both the good and the bad things in our lives can hold us down. Both good and bad circumstances can become familiar and comfortable. We get used to the things we deal with every day.

Life can be so good we don't want to rock the boat.
Life can be so hard we can't seem to break out of the
cycles of despair and debt, or we can't see any
way out.

The only question that matters is *how long do you want to keep letting whatever it is that is holding you down, hold you down?* How long do you want to give up your power? You have the ability to change your dynamics, the way you think and live, and the success you can achieve. And yes, it's a decision. It isn't like a fairy god-mother with a magic wand . . . it may take some time. For some, longer than others. How long do you want to hang onto the past and to things that have held you back up until now? Forgive the bad, and move on.

What Is Your Reality?

Your mind is powerful, powerful, *powerful!* Most people use less than 10 percent of what they've got up there. Only God knows what all the rest is doing, but I can tell you this much: Our realities are what we perceive them to be. Our mind creates the world in which we choose to live.

Scientists years ago did an experiment with fish to see just how far behavior can be ingrained, even in the face of a different reality. They put a big fish into a tank and fed him all the minnows he wanted—his favorite food. After a couple of days, they slid a glass divider into the tank, and put the minnows on the other side of the glass. The big fish charged at the minnows, slamming into the glass. He was stunned, but still hungry, so he slammed again and again. After several hours of this, he stopped trying and nursed his sore nose.

The scientists waited for a couple of days, but the big fish didn't move an inch. So they pulled out the glass divider. Pretty soon, the minnows were swimming all over the tank, right in front of the big fish's nose. Man, food was everywhere, but the big fish never tried to eat them. He had been so conditioned that he would slam into the wall if he went for the minnows that he stayed there until he died of starvation, with dozens of minnows all around him.

That fish was living in the past. He was living by a memory that had been forced on him. He died because he couldn't get past that memory, that past hurt. Fish are much simpler animals than humans. He became hardwired to sit there in his nice, safe corner. His fish brain had figured out that if he just sat still, and didn't *try* anymore, he wouldn't get hurt. And so he waited, until he starved to death. But you are not a fish. You have a brain, an intellect, and a will. Are you going to let past hurts and slights, past failures, determine your future?

> *The same attitude and behavior exists in people—*
> *maybe you can even see it in your own life. You may*
> *be surrounded by opportunity but have become*
> *convinced, in your mind, that it's not for you, that if*
> *you try, you don't stand a chance.*

We've talked about people who've been abused by a parent, a spouse, or someone else. We all know people in these situations, and some are still suffering. They can even continue to suffer long after their abuser is gone, in prison, or dead. Why? Their tormentor is no longer around. The person who hurt them no longer has any degree of actual control over them. Their suffering today is all in their mind, their memories, their emotions.

As a man thinks in his heart, so is he.

—*Proverbs 3:27*

Please don't blow this scripture off. Forgiveness is too important to dismiss that easily. God gave us the choice of what we think, feel, and believe—and the degree of control we let others have in our life. I have that choice. You do, too. And you can change your decisions at any time, to make new choices for better or for worse. It's up to you.

Decisiveness and Determination

One of the key elements we've talked about is the ability to make decisions. It may be safe to act like the fish and just decide not to decide, not to act. But as we've seen, indecisiveness is a decision all by itself. Not showing up for the game means you choose to lose the game, by default. And unfortunately, that's how way too many lives play out—by default.

Successful people have to make decisions, every day. And some of those decisions will be bad ones. The person in the abusive relationship made a bad decision. But that doesn't mean she has to keep on living that out. She has the power to make a new decision.

I've made business decisions before that looked real good. Later, as more information became available, I realized some weren't so good after all. Time to change. Time to make a new decision for a new direction, and move on.

Sometimes a past decision and its consequences are things we can't just "walk away from." Like having a baby. I see young men just walk away from their responsibility, and young girls letting their mother or grandmother raise their kids. They made a bad decision, maybe just a default decision in the heat of the moment, but it was their decision all the way. The kid who shoplifts or gets into drugs has made decisions, and those have consequences, too. If I buy a company or a house and find out it has all sorts of issues and problems, I may not be able to just make an easy change, but I have to find a way to deal with the consequences. That's all part of life and being empowered. Sometimes we have to learn to move on in spite of the consequences, even when it means lugging those concrete blocks down the field in the process. My point is: This is *your* life. Victims don't take the responsibility but spend their time blaming and complaining. Winners take it on the chin and keep moving forward.

To be an empowered person means you recognize you can make your own decisions. Victims have given their power to someone else, and that other person or persons run their life. When I depend on some government program to feed and clothe me, to put a roof over my head, I'm at the mercy of some bureaucrat in an office somewhere to handle it all. I give up my power and let him make all the decisions.

Some people like this, and some don't. It's easier to complain when the plumbing is stopped up and call someone else to take care of the problem. It's more of a challenge to handle my own stopped-up toilet and clean up my own mess. But I can make the decision to do it, or get it done right away. By the time the government or land-lord processes my paperwork, I may not be able to stay in the house because of the smell!

All that control we want in our life, all that empowerment, means we have to take a stand. What are your dreams? You know now there's always a cost. How much are your dreams worth to you? Are you willing to draw a line in the sand and say, "This is what I want in my life?"

Setting goals means making decisions. Do you want to go to college? Do you want to start a business? Do you want to pursue art or see the world? What do you want? Only you can decide.

In business and in life, nobody can make your decisions for your future better than you. I'll get some flak for this but this includes your parents. They don't have to live out your life. You do. However, if you want to run your life, don't expect your parents to come along and clean up all your messes, either. Decisiveness means taking responsibility. If your decisions are bad, you may have consequences to deal with. But make up your mind that it's better to try something great and fail, than to attempt nothing and succeed at nothing.

Sticking with Your Decisions

When you make a decision, you may find that the path you've chosen isn't the one you want to stay on. This is only natural. We grow, we change, we get new information. You have that right. But just like with a business plan, this is also a crucial point where your ability to be honest with yourself and not use excuses or fear as your motivation is most important. Sometimes we have to deal with the decisions we have already made as we choose new directions. It may take years longer for the single mom with a baby to go back to school, to get the education she may need to reach her dream, but the important thing is that she keeps moving ahead anyway.

Your willpower is important in any decision. Otherwise, you'll be moved this way and that, listening to other people's opinions and warnings. It's important to keep your eyes on the goal, your prize, your treasure, and run the race. Like everything else we've talked about, willpower is something in your mind, an act of your will. You have the power—it comes from the inside out; it's already there.

Making quality decisions is not always easy; in fact, it's downright hard a lot of times. But make your decision and go with it. Don't change directions just because it's hard, or you find it overwhelming at times. Don't give into excuses. Forgive those hurts and move on. Stare down your fears and everything else that sucks the power out of your life. And you will find that power inside. You will feel the rush. Empowerment. It's how God meant life to be for all of us.

Ultimately, the difference between being a victim controlled by others and a nonvictim walking in power lies in how you choose to react to the things that happen to you. The proactive person chooses to move forward. She does not allow her power to be usurped by others. She makes the tough decisions when it comes to admitting her own shortcomings, but she uses this to improve and adapt. And she learns how to forgive.

This is what I would wish for you, my challenge to you: Never be a victim and enjoy the journey of your life every step of the way living a successful, empowered life.

Take Up the Challenge!

A lot of kids seem to think that the only way to get a lot of money—other than drugs and illegal stuff—is to be a hip hop star or do pro sports. You don't have to know much English—you can even talk street slang all the time. But most of those stars don't have any real money. It's the guys behind the scenes—their managers and financial advisors, their lawyers, and the record companies—who really have the money. A lot of the cool cars and stuff they have are rented or leased. When they show up at some awards ceremony with a million dollars worth of bling on—gold, platinum, diamonds, and such—it isn't even theirs. It's just rented or borrowed for the evening. Then, like Cinderella, at midnight they have to give it back. But that's not the image that's being portrayed out there. We're doing "show and tell" every day with our youth, telling them this is how they have to be to have all that wealth that they see. And it's all a lie. But the trouble is, if you believe in the lie, but can't make it real, what then?

Real, Real World

Kids who have been brainwashed with mass media fantasies need a dose of reality. Not reality-show reality but the kind that normal, successful people live. A great example of this can be seen in the daily work of organizations like FAMLI in Los Angeles, which my company, City Capital, supports. FAMLI's "See a Man, Be a Man" and "From Princess to Queen" mentorship programs teach young people simple concepts like cleanliness, responsibility, respect for girls and their families, and the importance of education. Founder and CEO Torrénce Brannon Reese was a program director for the LA Bridges gang prevention program, and has been voted one of the "Top 100 Most Important People in Los Angeles" by the *LA Times* and *LA Watts Times*, among loads of other honors. Torré tells his students to "Stop thinking about the bling all the time! The odds are you'll never have a shot at being a pro athlete or hip hop singer. You've gotta have a backup plan." But the bling is still all they see.

FAMLI operates in one of the roughest areas of Southwest LA. Torré holds after-school classes at Audubon Middle School in Liemert Park. According to FAMLI, out of all 78 middle schools in the LA United School District, Audubon has the second-highest percentage of students without fathers.

Eighty-five percent of Torré's students come from single-parent households headed by women, and 90 percent lack any viable male role models. These are the kind of kids I've been talking about. They're sixth and seventh graders, the same age I was when I started my first business. These are the ones who are most at risk for gang violence, drug abuse, gangbanging, jail time, and death. The same things that influence them affect all kids and young people today.

But Torré won't give up. He had to put his kids on city buses 5 or 10 at a time just to go on an outing to a swimming pool or museum. Not too many at a time because the bus drivers didn't want any discipline problems. So it could take an hour or more, just to get them all a couple of miles. That's why, in 2006, City Capital purchased a 15-passenger van for Torré and his kids. Here's what Torré shared at the time:

> *In the midst of a nation of people who seem to lack direction and focus, Ephren Taylor is singularly focused on solutions. The fact he has not yet reached the age of 25 is all the more compelling, as his youthfulness presents us all with an opportunity to dream and have hope again.*
>
> *Specifically, he is in the tradition of Booker T. Washington, Marcus Garvey, and the black people who built those great institutions such as the Negro National Baseball League; people like Andrew "Rube" Foster, Oscar Micheaux, and so many others. He is a living example for our youth today.*

Time for a Change

I've never tried to hold myself up as better than anyone else. I know my talents, and I've been blessed to be able to use my success to spread a positive message to young people all over the country. What we need are more Torrés out there, working in the trenches. We need more committed people working face-to-face with kids in the hood.

My hope with the Urban Wealth Tour is to raise more leaders like these in every city. We have to change the negative images out there. Change some of the thought processes and expand these kids' visions into the world of real opportunity all around them. Torré called me an example for our youth. National radio host Tom Joyner called me "Living Black History." Sometimes praise like this can get to be a little much, but if I can make some history in terms of bringing people up, I'll take that accolade.

My only desire is that I'm able to get in front of enough kids so they can see somebody who came from the same situation as they did, looks like they do—and who made it anyway. Not as some loudmouth superstar with lots of status symbol bling, but someone real who started with little and who did real things to make it big. So they can make it, too. And if we can get enough of these kinds of images and examples out there, so that it doesn't seem like I'm such an isolated case, we can change lives. We'll change communities, our country, and the world. But right now, I'm still an exception to what the statistics say.

Get Uncomfortable and Face Your Fears

I believe that if there is any secret to success, it is creating a habit of making yourself *uncomfortable*.

Our mental image of super-success may be some rich fat-cat lazing by the pool in some tropical paradise, smoking a stogie, sipping little drinks with umbrellas, with not a care in the world. A lot of people have similar images about retirement, maybe without all the money but being able to take it easy . . . you know, "gone fishing."

The reality is living the "no worries" lifestyle will kill us. We all know being a couch potato creates major medical and physical problems that can destroy us. In the same way, staying in a place where we're mentally comfortable all the time destroys our ability to achieve our dreams. Just like the sirens of Greek mythology, our Comfort Zone lulls us and we end up dashing our ship against the rocks of failure.

A Comfort Zone Is Nothing But a Prison without Walls

When people tell me something makes them uncomfortable, or it's outside their Comfort Zone, I usually say, "Great!" If I want to build a muscle, the only way I can do it is to become uncomfortable or to go outside my normal zone. I may like lying on the couch watching football games and reruns, sucking down sodas, and grubbing on potato chips, but to get strong I have to go to the gym. And then I have to pump iron, sweat off the fat, and push myself past my comfort limits. In other words, I have to get uncomfortable and just deal with what has to be done to reach my goal.

We feel safe in our Comfort Zone. We feel anxious whenever we move beyond it or get pushed out of it. The trouble is our fears are always out there circling around us, like wolves circling a campsite. We build our walls, our "ring of fire" to keep them out, but they're always just beyond the ring, just waiting for us to slip outside, so they can pounce on us. Our fears have teeth and snarl at us whenever we start to stretch ourselves even a little bit. But we can't live a full life if we stay inside that circle, the Comfort Zone, all of our life.

> *Walls keep danger out, but they keep our potential locked away.*

Our fears aren't really wolves circling around us. They're right there inside that circle with us every moment of our lives. They're inside us, inside our heads, and they rule our lives and how far we can go. Or we rule them. They can't really eat us, and they *can* be overcome, but *only* by doing the things we fear most. And that is always going to be uncomfortable.

We have to be willing to take on our fears one by one. We have to challenge our fears. We have to beat them, or they will dominate us and ruin our lives. We have to force ourselves to move outside the circle—*out of our Comfort Zone*—and face our fears head-on. And if we falter, we get back up and do it again, and again, as many times as necessary . . . until we dominate our fears.

Nobody has ever lived completely without fear, except perhaps Jesus. And even He had to face the onslaught of thoughts that would have kept him safe in the garden, surrounded by friends, instead of taking on those thoughts and facing them. The Bible says he sweated as though it were great drops of blood. Sweating blood. Sweating bullets. But not backing down. Stepping out in faith.

Fear cripples us; faith empowers us.

Every time we tackle one fear and overcome it, we have another one to face, and the process starts all over again. We may never be free from all fear, but we don't have to be a slave to any fears in our life either. Once you know this secret, once you get it, fear can never again hold you back—unless you allow it to.

Don't think of this as one endless struggle, one that we must simply endure. Instead, think of it as one triumph after another, from peak to peak, from mountaintop to mountaintop. And yes, I still have fears, many fears. But I am constantly reminded of this scripture:

> Greater is He that is in you, than He that is in the world!
>
> —*1 John 4:4*

The uncomfortable truth is you can never be successful as long as you allow yourself to stay comfortable. A "comfortable" income will only keep you from striving for more . . . ask any sales manager. That manager wants hungry salespeople, not satisfied cows waiting for the next buyer to stumble into their trough.

Having some passive, "I don't care, whatever, it's okay with me" attitude can also lead to a sense of resentment and contempt within our relationships. Just being too comfortable in a relationship can ultimately lead to a break up and divorce. When we allow ourselves to feel too relaxed, like we don't have to do anything to make it keep working day by day, we start taking things for granted. Relationships take a lot of work. Businesses take a lot of work. Investments need constant attention. Dreams must be pursued actively, intently, or they'll slip away in front of you . . . always just out of reach.

The Apostle Paul, who by anyone's reckoning lived a life that was anything *but* comfortable, said,

> I have learned in whatever state I am, to be content.
>
> —*Philippians 4:11*

Contentment is not the same as comfortable. His life was not one of apathy, indifference, or laziness . . . in fact, he was in prison when he wrote this letter. So how does this jive with getting outside of our Comfort Zone? Simple. Paul wasn't agitated and nervous, worrying and fretting all the time. He took it all in stride. He was content; he was happy. He was living his passion. Nothing else around him—not people, not circumstances—changed his goal or his vision. Paul continually pushed himself out of any normal human being's Comfort Zone, yet he was okay with what that meant in his life. His conclusion shows his confidence that whatever obstacles came his way, he would be able to overcome and reach his goals.

> I can do all things through Christ which strengtheneth me.
>
> —*Philippians 4:13*

The Only Way to True Contentment Is to Keep Yourself Uncomfortable

It's the difference between the athlete who has chosen to go for the gold, to spend hours of focus and effort every day for their goal and the average person trying to fit a few minutes of exercise into their life. The athlete isn't comfortable; in fact, he spends a lot of his time in physical pain, always pushing the envelope. But he is content.

He has focus, passion. "No pain, no gain," really means something to them. *They don't live for the pain; they live for the dream.*

On the other hand, we (and I include myself in this) who half-heartedly run some laps or lift some weights occasionally, are not only outside our Comfort Zones, we're pretty miserable in our discontent. I personally would rather sleep after a great Thanksgiving meal than jog around the block or go to the gym. I know "no pain" means "I gain—weight," but I have no passion for exercise. It's an area that I constantly wrestle with. It is my bed of nails, my thorn in the flesh. I know what I need to do, but it's still a struggle.

Yet, I know that this is an area I have to force myself outside of my Comfort Zone. By allowing myself to stay in my Comfort Zone, I'll die early and my kids will be left fatherless. For me, it is totally about disciplining myself, about making and sticking with my decision. I do it every day in business, and I succeed. I will fight to succeed at the physical side of my life as well.

Unlike my struggle to stay physically fit, most of the major success decisions in my life have bucked the trend of what people all around me were saying and doing. I didn't earn the Young Entrepreneur of the Year award because I was doing business like everyone else. I know I can have no success in any area of my life, until I'm willing to get out of my Comfort Zone. Very often, the decisions to move out of our Comfort Zones mean going against Conventional Wisdom.

Conventional Wisdom Is Almost Always Wrong

When I began working with churches, helping them build their endowment programs, everyone else was telling them to play it safe, put their money in CDs and money market accounts. I made a bold proposition to the church boards: Why not take the same money, invest in the communities and people around you? Why not rehab or build affordable homes for families? *Why not give?*

By the way, not only is it *not* wrong to expect a return on an investment—even our giving—but in some places the Bible infers it may be a sin not to have a positive expectation and faith that your "sowing" will reap rewards. The faithful servant in one parable (Matthew 25) was honored for investing this way, expecting a return, while his fellow servants who "played it safe" were really scolded.

> Give, and it shall be given unto you; Full measure, pressed down, shaken together, running over . . .
>
> —*Luke 6:38*

So much of what we're talking about flies in the face of Conventional Wisdom. But if you follow "normal" thinking, you'll make pretty common decisions that will result in a mediocre life. How can I say this? Let's use my area of business expertise as an example. Most businesses, some say as many as 97 out of 100, fail in the first three years. Most of their owners are probably making pretty normal decisions, but their decisions are all based on Conventional Wisdom. And the numbers prove that this is a fatal mistake.

To their credit, these business owners have pushed through many of their excuses and fears and actually opened their own business. They've set up shop, ordered inventory, and made sure they're in the Yellow Pages. But most still fail, miserably. They crawl away from the table of success with their tail between their legs. And yet, they did everything that common understanding told them to do. What went wrong? To get an answer, let's look at some of the "Conventional Wisdom" advice people have given me as I've built City Capital:

- To make the most money, developers should build expensive high-dollar homes and huge resorts and golf course developments. That's where the money is. Don't invest in urban markets because they are "war zones." But we found a tremendous need and desire in these markets, and very little competition when we provide quality homes for working-class families.

- You should be satisfied with a low—3 percent, 4 percent, or 5 percent—return on your investments because the lower the return, the safer the investment. *It's better to be safe than sorry.* According to this theory, the only way to get high returns is to increase risk. But we found our government partners more than willing to help offset many of the risks because of the great need for affordable homes and renewable fuels.

- When you're negotiating with someone, they're your opponent, and you've got to negotiate from a "position of strength." But we have found that by approaching all negotiations in a win-win manner, other parties cooperate with us and give us great incentives to work with them.

- You can't get financing, you can't get qualified buyers, you can't afford to market, you can't do something new, you can't, you can't, you can't . . . I've said it before, I always look for the "I can" and I usually find it.

I've been given all these dire warnings and many more based on Conventional Wisdom. I never automatically assumed they were correct, and neither should you. We at City Capital took a whole different approach and went way outside the box.

City Capital approaches cities and communities with an attitude of giving. We ask them "What do you need for your people? What would you like to see provided? What kind of community do you envision?" That may not sound too radical, but believe me, from what economic development groups and community development corporations tell us, we are often the only organization that has ever approached them this way. If we hadn't, we'd have been no different than all the companies out there who try to put the squeeze on cities and make the big bucks. We've found that our approach is so unique among developers that other companies are more than happy to pay to have us put together the agreements while they carry out the developments.

Our biofuels division, Goshen Energy Resources, has approached the renewable energy market the same way. We have found that a lot of different governmental and private groups have a lot of interest in the future of this important field. However, most groups aren't included in the "big deal" conversations that are taking place. We are finding partners with universities, Native Americans, distribution companies, and local and state governments. Our win-win approach is opening new doors of opportunity for the growth of our company in the United States, Africa, and other parts of the world.

You Can't Do That

I can't tell you how many hundreds of times I've been told "You can't do that" over the years. Probably more than most people because I've attempted to do things most people won't, at earlier ages than usual. It's not what you *can't* do that counts anyway; it's what you *can* do.

It Couldn't Be Done

Somebody said that it couldn't be done,
But he with a chuckle replied
That "maybe it couldn't," but he would be one
Who wouldn't say so till he'd tried.
So he buckled right in with the trace of a grin
On his face. If he worried he hid it.
He started to sing as he tackled the thing
That couldn't be done, and he did it.
Somebody scoffed: "Oh, you'll never do that;
At least no one ever has done it";
But he took off his coat and he took off his hat,
And the first thing we knew he'd begun it.
With a lift of his chin and a bit of a grin,
If any doubt rose he forbid it.
He started to sing as he tackled the thing
That couldn't be done, and he did it.
There are thousands to tell you it cannot be done,
There are thousands to prophesy failure;
There are thousands to point out to you, one by one,
The dangers that wait to assail you.
But just buckle in with a bit of a grin,
Just take off your coat and go to it;
Just start to sing as you tackle the thing
That "cannot be done," and you'll do it.

—Edgar Guest

I have very often gone against Conventional Wisdom in my decisions. And yet, since 1999, I've done what people said "cannot be done," like proving that investing in affordable single-family homes in primarily urban markets can create consistently high returns on investment for our investors. Or proving that a young, minority-owned, upstart, company could enter the biofuels business and succeed. In fact, sometimes just the fact that something doesn't fit Conventional Wisdom is enough reason to seriously consider it. If most people are following the mob reasoning, what opportunities are they missing along the way?

Remember that the mob is *always* following Conventional Wisdom. One of the great sayings in the stock market (and other markets) is, "Buy when there's blood in the streets." What does this mean? It means that when everyone is running the other way, swim upstream. When the mob is selling off their stocks cheaply, most other investors get nervous and start selling theirs off, too. Like a herd of animals cutting their losses and getting out while they can. That drives down stock prices and that's when the savvy investors start buying like crazy.

The qualities that allow us to succeed aren't all totally unique. All we have to do is buck the mob mentality—the Conventional Wisdom— to rebel against the people who would hold us back, and say "No!" to our fears. But be aware. The mob may ultimately laugh at your dream and intone the biggest Conventional Wisdom knock-out excuse of all: **"If it's so good, why isn't everyone doing it?"** To which I usually respond: **"Do highly successful people get there doing what everybody else does?"**

Most often the answer is "No!" This is what allows a handful of decisive individuals to make significant profits. In fact, it's estimated that about 7.3 million of these high net worth folks are millionaires, about a third of those are in the United States alone. And according to *Forbes* magazine, there are over 374 *billionaires* in the United States. These people aren't a million times smarter than you, and they don't work a million times harder than you . . . in fact, you probably work harder! So why do they make millions more dollars than you? Because they don't yield to fears, they don't accept excuses, and they don't rely on the mob's Conventional Wisdom.

Often, when I feel torn about a decision—should I do this, or should I do that?—I have learned to recognize that if I have the necessary information (from my people or outside sources) to make the decision but I'm still wavering, most often than not it's about me, something inside me. If I'm listening to the voice of Conventional Wisdom, I'm not thinking outside-the-box and seeing the other possibilities that always exist.

In cases like this, I have only one gear: *Forward, full speed ahead!* When I recognize that it's some fear deep within me trying to keep me from doing a deal, *I do the deal*. Period. Positive, appropriate action is the surest cure for indecisiveness. And remember, decisiveness is one of the primary keys of success . . . and the only way to use it is to *decide to!*

Whatever You Do, Make the Decision *to Take Positive, Appropriate Action to Move Forward. Be* Decisive!

See, the choice really is yours to make. Do you want to live in fear, in lack, following the mob and making decisions not to lose? Or do you want to overcome your fears, live in abundance, and make positive decisions to win? These are the choices we all have to make. And more often than not, the greatest decisions of your life, the ones that propel you further along than any others, are the ones that will fly in the face of Conventional Wisdom and push you outside of your Comfort Zone.

SECTION V

Why Every Young Person Should Start a Business

The idea of opening and running your own business can be a scary one. "Who, *me*?" Sure, there are risks involved. But it can also be exciting and exhilarating. Just take a minute to imagine how cool it would be to be your own boss, setting the direction and calling the shots. Here are more great reasons to abandon your fear of starting and to help you kick start your own business right now:

1. *You have* nothing *to lose.* Look, the vast majority of people my age earn minimum wage. You're worth a whole lot more than $6 or $8 an hour. The worst thing that can happen if your business fails is that you have to go out and find a job. *Hello!?* If you decide to wait around and *not* go after your dream, you *still* have to get a job!

2. *You gain invaluable experience and credentials.* Owning and running a business will increase your chances of success in the future, no matter what kind of work you go into. You develop more of the "big picture" view, with more of an understanding of how all the pieces fit together to make the whole thing work . . . and you gain some great skills to list on your resume.

3. *Your chances of making a lot of money are far greater* . . . and chances are you'll make it a whole lot sooner. Even though less than 20 percent of American workers are self-employed, two-thirds of all millionaires are entrepreneurs, according to Stanley and Danko in *The Millionaire Next Door* (New York: Pocket Books, 1996). The income you earn is only part of it: If you sell a successful business or go public, you could have the biggest payday of your life.

4. *You get to make the rules.* You don't have to dance to anyone else's tune. You can create your own hours, work from wherever you want, and choose who you want to work with. You can pick what interests you most and build a business around it.

5. *You develop networking skills.* By running a business and being in the business community, you develop excellent contacts that

will open up all sorts of great new opportunities for you. Some contacts will even become lifelong mentors. *Your network increases your net worth.*

6. *You will learn more about yourself.* By running a business, you will learn what they don't teach you in school, including courage, strength, resilience, and determination.

7. *You're guaranteed employment.* The owners are the last people to go down with the ship if business turns bad. If you're an employee, your income is at the mercy of the boss . . . guess which one keeps getting a paycheck right up until the end.

So what *do* you want? What are the things you love, that you have passion about? When you're creating your own business, you have the choice to do what you love, so why not make it fun? The happiest people, the ones I consider most successful, are the ones that love what they do, and do what they love. Like everything else, it's your choice.

I Just Don't Know What I Want to Do

People who know where they are going are nearly unstoppable. Guys like Ray Kroc (McDonald's), Bill Gates (Microsoft), John Johnson (*Ebony* magazine), Kemmons Wilson (Holiday Inn), Charles Culpepper (Coca-Cola), or Sam Walton (Wal-Mart)—all had a singular vision and the drive to make it happen. They were like a bullet: focused on their target and moving ahead fast.

Madam C. J. Walker is listed in *Guinness Book of World Records* (London: Guinness World Records, 2003) as the first self-made woman millionaire in America—and she was black. She didn't take excuses from anybody, especially herself:

> *I am a woman who came from the cotton fields of the South. From there I was promoted to the washtub. From there I was promoted to the*

cook kitchen. And from there I promoted myself into the business of manufacturing hair goods and preparations. . . . I have built my own factory on my own ground.

You can find examples of success all around you. Regardless of your interests or the career you want to pursue, you can find people who have succeeded. And if they're still alive, you can probably get in to see them and talk with them, and maybe even find a mentor or two.

People who have this kind of single mindedness are bound to achieve their goals. Unfortunately, a lot of young people I talk to, people in their teens and twenties like me, seem to have no direction at all. They say, "I don't know what to do with my life."

Lack of Direction Stops You before You Begin

My suspicion is that people who have no goals—no direction—have spent too much time being passive and letting everything happen *to* them. They're used to getting by. They passively listen to the teacher at school, they passively sit in front of their video game watching the screen and reacting when necessary; they passively watch TV; they passively listen to music or watch sports.

Their most serious planning goes into attracting the opposite sex so they can hook up. Even then, a lot of young people want to accomplish their romantic conquest with a minimum amount of effort. I'm not saying all kids are like this nor am I saying they're bad people. It's just that after all this "just getting by," they find it hard to look ahead and plan a career without someone telling them what they should do.

Many of the problems with out-of-wedlock babies and broken marriages is rooted in this passiveness. It takes work to build a relationship. It takes focus and caring about someone other than ourselves. It takes seeing the bigger picture, dealing with our own fears and excuses, and committing ourselves to making it work.

It takes everything we've been talking about, and more. You can't passively have a good relationship anymore than you can passively do a great job or build a great business. It takes focus, action, and determination to succeed. A lot of people think this is just too much work. They want an easy way to the easy life.

I see these same people as employees, spending more time planning their annual vacation than they spend planning their finances. Can we say "priorities" here? Take the time to figure out what you really want and then make a plan to go for it.

Start with What You Know

My best advice is still to go with what you love to do. If you do what you love, you'll never have a job, right? I was just a kid who was crazy about video games, remember? I couldn't get enough of them. I always had my face in a video screen, and I spent thousands of hours playing video games. As a result, the idea of creating my own video game or starting a web site grew naturally out of something I was already passionate about.

I loved doing that business. Along the way I found other things I loved doing that I could make money at, too. Once I tasted success as my own boss, how could I ever work for someone else in my life? Was it work? No way! I enjoyed every minute of the process and the money I made was just icing on the cake.

When It's Your Passion, It's Not Work

Every day I drive past a cul-de-sac where some kids have set up a ramp and a quarter-pipe so they can skateboard. They're out there every morning before school, practicing hour after hour so they can perfect their flips, turns, and other stunts. Every night when I'm driving home I see them. They're still out there, under a streetlight, jumping, flipping, falling, crashing. They sweat, strain, and endure endless scrapes, bruises, and cuts in pursuit of mastering the board. They will try a trick, fall down on the asphalt (hard!), get up, and try it again. If they get hurt, they get a bandage or a cast, wait awhile, and go back to do it again.

These kids put out more physical—and mental—effort in this than they do all day at school. But, do you think they consider it work? Of course not! It's what they *live* for. At the end of the day, their exhaustion and pain is mixed with a feeling of satisfaction and inner happiness that they've moved another step closer to achieving a personal goal. Some of these kids have gone on to become professionals in the sport, others have fine-tuned the equipment, designed their own boards, started their own skateboard parks, traveled around writing about boarding, and on and on. One thing I know for sure: none of them considers all that work, as *work*. It's not a job; it's their passion.

It's no good having material success if you have no passion for the work you do. What kind of enjoyment can come from the drudgery of doing something you don't like, so that you can enjoy some fleeting moments with "the lifestyle?" That sounds too much like a job to me. In fact, let's look at that word *work*. You'll find that successful people honestly don't even consider what they do to be work—it's their *passion*, their source of energy, even their mission. They get excitement from what they do and it gives them a great amount of pleasure. I know it's true for me.

> *Every day I wake up with my head full of plans and ideas. I go to work and meet with people I respect and admire. But most of all I love the process of taking an idea and making it become reality.*

I love finding ways to blend traditional nonprofit activities with our "for profit" business. I believe every corporation should be expected to give back, to be socially-conscious in whatever work they do. For instance, at City Capital, we are constantly reviewing proposals from cities to revitalize one of their urban neighborhoods. Taking a run-down area, turning it into new homes and businesses, and providing affordable homes to working-class families who deserve them is one way to empower communities.

I've already talked some about City Capital's Goshen Energy Resources division and our plans to develop biofuels. I get so excited I can hardly stand it—to think that we're doing energy deals. When we closed on our first property, I e-mailed the "Beverly Hillbillies" theme song to all my staff around the country. I can't imagine doing stuff and having any more fun than the things I'm doing right now. Work? I don't know the meaning of the word! Where there's passion, there is no work because every effort is an act of love.

Remember in *Back to the Future* where they put garbage in the car to make it run? We're doing that right now on a prototype scale using garbage, grease from wastewater treatment plants, wood chips from dead trees, cow flop, you name it! We're also developing partnerships and testing different types of plants to create biodiesel and other renewable fuels.

Cities, states, and even countries are already talking to us about having this cutting-edge technology to benefit their people. Using garbage and other waste products to make diesel and other fuels.

Developing these processes has become a new passion for me. It's not only a wide-open field, it's one more way we can help people become more self-sufficient and empowered . . .

What Are You Passionate About?

You don't have to limit yourself to something you are currently skilled at—*it's more important that you have a passion that will drive you.* Perhaps you've always admired the way welders can make practically anything out of steel. Even if you have never held a welding torch in your hand, it's a goal you can pursue. Like the open road? Like styling your friends' hair and doing makeup? There are training schools across the country where you can learn these trades while getting leads for dozens of jobs and freelance work. Sure, you'll need to save up money to attend, but a lot of them have scholarship and student loan programs. If that's what you want to do, go for it. Once you get the training, you can use your new skills in many ways, not just working at a job. With any of these, you can run your own show, too.

If you can't think of anything you're passionate about, you might need to do some serious "prospecting." By that I mean you may have to look around a bit and find something that you think you might enjoy *and* make money doing. Here's a formula that is tried and true and has been used by successful entrepreneurs forever:

Find a need and fill it.

All you have to do is look around your neighborhood or your city. Think about what people are doing and how you could help them.

Are there many older people in your neighborhood? Perhaps they need someone who can do their shopping for them.

Are there many single mothers where you live? One of their biggest needs is finding someone who can watch the kids while they go shopping, go to the doctor, go to dinner, or visit friends. That's a service you could provide. And what about when they go on vacation? You could get paid for staying in their house, eating their food, and watching their widescreen television . . . not too shabby.

One of my first businesses was based on a need that was right in front of me—teenagers needing jobs. I knew this because most of my friends were looking for summer jobs. I figured there also had to be some employers and businesspeople out there who needed young employees on a part-time or full-time basis. So, being the computer nerd that I was, I knew there had to be a way to use the Internet to match up those employers with kids looking for work. That's when I got the idea for GoferretGo.com. The web site matched kids with jobs and employers with employees. It was a natural fit for me, and a great success as a business. In fact, it became one of the top teen-owned companies in the country, ranked Number 4 by *YoungBiz* magazine.

Go Ahead, Get Creative

One of the things I love to do is look around and figure out business opportunities wherever I happen to be. It's this game I play in my mind, to keep on the cutting edge. I might drive by a bus stop and see a group of folks waiting there. Every day, all day long, there are groups of 10 to 15 people at those bus stop locations. It reminds me of when I was in elementary school and would carry pencils and things out to recess to sell to the kids standing around. What if I had a way to sell snacks and drinks, or magazines and newspapers, to those people while they're waiting? What if I had a van that could go to all the bus stops in the city . . . one big route over and over? Is there money in that? I don't know, but it's an idea. If it worked, I wouldn't even have to drive the van. I could hire someone else to run the routes for me.

Have you ever had to wait and wait in a doctor's office? Sometimes I wait for over an hour. It drives me crazy. People waiting in doctors' offices are a captive audience. What if I installed a video system in those offices with my own programs and advertising? People might be willing to pay for ads on that video system. This is the way my mind works. I'm always coming up with ideas. Some of them work out well. Some (like this one for doctors' offices), I've seen developed by others. That just goes to show you, ideas have merit.

> I really don't think life is about the I-could-have-beens. Life is only about the I-tried-to-do's. I don't mind the failure but I can't imagine that I'd forgive myself if I didn't try.
>
> —*Nikki Giovanni*

Your search for a business might turn up a product that needs to be invented—like a do-it-yourself kit that lets kids retread their favorite athletic shoes to make them last longer. Now what parent wouldn't want to buy a kit for $24.95 after forking out $100 or $200 for a pair of designer shoes?

It's like that *Back to the Future* example I gave awhile back. It sounded crazy for the professor to replace the fusion reactor in the car with tone that ran on garbage, but now we're doing just that. Next time you watch some wild sci-fi movie, pay closer attention. Someone else's crackpot idea might be your key to financial success.

Don't Assume an Idea Won't Work

This really drives home that you should never assume your ideas are crazy, no matter what anybody tells you. Maybe some are, but if there's a real need out there, money can be made by someone with the vision. Will it be you? I'm always amazed at the junk people are pushing on those late-night infomercials and shop-at-home channels. It blows my mind, and reminds me that any idea deserves to be looked at carefully. There are no stupid ideas or questions.

However, let's stop for just a minute and talk about how your idea becomes a business. There are a lot of people whose passion is playing a guitar. I see them all the time in parks and on street corners, with a tin can or old hat for tips. That's not the kind of business I'm talking about.

Just like you shouldn't assume your ideas are crazy, you can't automatically assume there *is* a market for your idea *just because it isn't being done*. That can be just as big a mistake.

For instance, in one city I was speaking in on our Urban Wealth Tour, we ate at a great Serbo-Croatian restaurant. We don't have any of these eateries near where I live. Could be a great opportunity! But just because there *isn't* one in my neighborhood doesn't mean that it would be an instant hit if you opened one. In fact, there may be very good reasons why there aren't any. It could be that most Americans haven't developed a taste for Serbo-Croatian food yet. Or it could be that the food preparation is just too expensive, requiring lots of imported food items that cut into profits. Or perhaps, some simple market research might show that only five Serbo-Croatians live within 10 miles of my house, and that's not nearly enough of an ethnic market base to support a start up.

I've been approached by four or five companies with a next generation super e-mail system, but I don't think any of them stand a chance against Microsoft. Now if you could invent an engine that runs on water—*there's* a need everyone wants to have filled.

If you've got an idea for a new product, or think you have a way to turn your passion into a business, go for it. But first, do a little research. Ask people if they would buy such a thing. Go online and do some market research on related products, see who leads the field, and if there are some products that do something similar. Make a prototype and see if it interests the typical user. In other words, do your due diligence. Some people are so scared they'll get rejected that they avoid asking these hard questions. Recognize that fear, and push through it. You need facts to back up your theory.

Don't fall so in love with your idea or business plan that you become blind to its flaws or ignore other ways it might work better. Remember our procrastinator trying to start a business? He never got off the "great idea" stage and wasn't able to adapt enough to even get it off the ground. He had loads of other options, ways he could have adapted his plan and had a successful business, but he only saw one way to plow ahead. And so things as simple as his boss expecting him to work all day instead of calling on banks (go figure!) were enough to keep him back.

So many business people cling to the "perfect" plan in their mind, unable to see the alternatives that could make it succeed. They doggedly push on, beating against the wall hoping the wall will move. It doesn't. They fail. And often, they were *that* close.

Going from passion to business plan is a major step. Gathering the information and knowledge you need to succeed will help ensure your success. And being willing to be flexible with your idea and plan will give you the winning edge.

Don't Wait until You're Old, or Even Grown Up

I really believe that all of my successes after starting Flame Software when I was 12 were partially the result of having seen that I could do it. In the beginning, we all have to start out on faith. But after awhile, we have more confidence that things will work out. That we'll know where to get the information and whatever else we need. And most of all, we trust that we will do whatever it takes, no matter what.

These are all real good reasons to start young, because the longer you wait, the harder it gets. What gets harder? Taking chances, doing risky things, going out on your own.

Unfortunately, everything around us says,
"Wait until you finish school . . . get a degree . . .

had 5 or 10 years of experience under your belt.
Wait until . . ."

The beauty of starting young is that you don't really know you can fail, and even if you do, it's not the end of the world. I mean, do you think those skateboarding kids worry a lot about surviving a head injury if they slip on a flip? No way! Because when we're young, we're indestructible. Stupid sometimes, because we just assume we won't fall. And if we do fall, we won't be hurt too bad. And if we are hurt, we figure we'll heal fast and do it again.

It's the same with a business. We still have our life ahead of us to try again, and again, however many times it takes to succeed. Besides, people in their teens and early twenties don't have that much to lose. We haven't bought houses or accumulated all the stuff people seem to collect through their lives. Someone who's married with a couple of kids, has a steady job, a house and a mortgage—that person has a lot on the line. They've got other people depending on them. They've got to think about protecting and taking care of their family and what they have. They're not free to go off and try some new venture that could risk everything. They may not be as willing to move, or travel, if that was what it took to make it work.

As a result, the older we get the more conservative and careful we tend to become. That's not to say it's impossible for older and more settled adults to dive into a new business and make it work. Can someone begin their own venture at age 30, 40, or even 50 or 60? Can you be too old? No. Age isn't the issue. But commitments and responsibilities can affect our decisions.

If you're a young person, I encourage you, *don't* let yourself get caught up in all the stuff of life, all the struggle to make ends meet, to study, to work, and to make your paycheck last from week to week. Don't start a family and buy expensive things with expensive monthly payments. Live so far under what you may be able to afford, that you can sack away some seed money for your own gig. Sure, you have to be responsible, but don't take on any more responsibilities and debts than you have to.

Youth Can Actually Be an Advantage

You have no idea how many people say to me, "If only I had had the sense to get started when I was your age . . ." I used to brush it off, you know, some sappy saying by old people. Like an empty compliment. Then I began to realize the wisdom that they were giving me. They were saying, "I missed it, but you're not! I didn't do it, but you are. Keep on keepin' on! You're on the right track, just don't quit." It was like instant validation of my dreams and goals.

Of course, some jobs or businesses may require a certification, a diploma, or an advanced degree. There's no question it takes time to acquire those things. There's nothing that says a kid in high school can't study medicine or law. I'm just talking about studying, not taking on patients. Why not start now? You could be years ahead of everyone else when you do attend medical school. You may even be able to test out of some of the courses in the first year or two.

When the book learning from all the technical manuals took me as far as I could go in computer programming, I took classes, too. Then I signed up for what my mom called "Bill Gates University" so I could take those intense crash courses and certifications. I did what it took, but I didn't stop everything else in my life. I just added it all on top. I spent hours every day playing video games before that, so why not use the time to grow and get the knowledge I needed to succeed?

I began my career at a very young age, basically because I didn't see any reason why I shouldn't. I went and got the training I needed to make it work. I didn't wait until I graduated from high school (or even middle school). I started right where I was. Some people told me I needed to wait. Some warned of terrible consequences, like grades dropping and losing my childhood, whatever that means. I'm glad I didn't listen. There was not one good reason not to get started then and there.

Knowledge is the prime need of the hour.

—*Mary Macleod Bethune*

In this quote, you notice Bethune, one of the founders of the highly rated Bethune-Cookman College in Florida, didn't say "parking your butt in a vinyl chair and slogging through some degree, just to be able to say you'd done it." She was talking about *knowledge*, and how important it is to obtain it.

I'm a big fan of schools like DeVry Institute, ITT Technical School, and University of Phoenix. These are schools that cut all the fat out of education and give you just the meat. If you want to learn electronics, they teach you electronics. If you want to learn computers, that's what you get. Your education takes a half or a third of the time and you end up with the solid knowledge you need to proceed.

A lot of people dismiss these kinds of schools, but when I see them on a resume it tells me something about the person more than just what they studied. It tells me *how* they studied, how focused they are, and how they think and act when they have a goal. It tells me they're go-getters, the kind of people I want to bring into our business because I know they're self-motivators who will do what it takes to get the job done.

Education *can* make us more successful in life, not because of the shingle on our wall, but because it helps us understand the world around us better. I find way too many young people thinking they need a college degree so they can become financially successful. Like somehow college equals being rich. I find too many adults thinking, "If I'd only gone to college . . ." and you know where that line of thought leads us—back into excuses again!

Please, don't write me and get down on me because you think I don't value higher education. I do. It's that whole "career path" thing and all the one-size-fits-all educational system that bothers me. We've come to equate college with business success. I've said it before: all education should enrich our lives, open new doors to the world, expand our understanding, and help us become "well-rounded," as my mother would say.

Remember, the knowledge itself isn't the power. It's the proper application of that knowledge that leads to success. Too often in modern education, there's this disconnect between the two.

True Success and Giving Back: What Is True Success?

Sometimes it is easier to talk about what success isn't, rather than what it is. Remember *The Millionaire Next Door?* Success is not about how much money you make or have in the bank, how big a house you live in, or the circles you run in. It's not about how many clubs you're a part of, how extravagant your parties are, or how lavish your vacations may be. It's not about being a workaholic, and it's not even really about reaching a point where you don't have to work at all.

Martin Luther King . . . was he a success? How about the Tuskegee Airmen? Albert Einstein? George Washington Carver? Were any of these men super successful? You sure can't point to their money for your answer. Did the fact that they didn't make a ton of money make them failures? Chumps? Stupid? *No way!*

Success Is More about Giving, than Getting

We've talked about having a giving attitude, instead of being someone always on the lookout for Number One. Someone who understood the giving concept intimately was World War I hero Sergeant Alvin York. When we opened our corporate offices in Franklin, Tennessee, I was reminded of Sergeant York. He's the state's "Favorite Son." They have built monuments to him, and even named a highway after him. I remember seeing the old black-and-white movie "Sergeant York" when I was a kid. He starts out as just a hillbilly, but when he went off to fight in World War I he saved his platoon and was awarded the Medal of Honor. York took out 32 German soldiers, knocked out 35 German machine guns, and captured 132 prisoners, single-handedly.

So what did Sergeant York do with all that success? I mean he had a ticker tape parade in Manhattan, he had book deals and movie deals and speaking engagements . . . you name it. Instant celebrity! He could have made a ton of money.

Instead, after he came home from the war, he used all the money he made to bring education to the poverty-stricken mountain kids in Tennessee. He didn't profit from any of it personally, but he is considered Tennessee's most beloved and successful citizen of all time. (Elvis may have more fans, but he's only a distant second to York when it comes to state pride in one of their "Favorite Sons.")

More than Skin Deep

Sure, we can usually assume someone is financially or socially successful from the outward trappings of his or her life, but these are really a small part of the overall picture. Our society tends to pay more attention to the financial superstars, but this has resulted in the "get all you can, and can all you get" philosophy. Besides, as I pointed out earlier, a lot of times the bling we see isn't even real. Superstars' limousines and mansions, even their clothes and jewelry, are often leased or rented, or provided by sponsors. Their managers and agents all take percentages—and everyone has a hand out. Most super-successful people don't waste their energy showing off their status symbols, they focus on enjoying their lives out of the limelight.

I have no qualms about making money. In fact, since my focus has been on building companies for over a dozen years, I've talked about making money to school and church groups all over America and all through this book. There is nothing wrong or evil about money. Everyone needs it; everyone uses it. Money is not good or evil. Even the Bible agrees with this—it's the *love* of money that's the root of all evil, not the money itself. And you don't have to have a penny to your name to be guilty of that sin.

Even though Jesus split up some loaves and fishes, someone bought the flour and baked the bread, they worked to get the fish or bought those, too, and gave them to him when he asked. God can multiply whatever you give, but you have to *have* to be willing to give. And usually, this takes money.

There's no shame in being poor, but there should be no pride in staying poor either, especially when there are so many opportunities for wealth. Poor people who can't save a dime can't feed refugee camps or build churches, schools, or orphanages. Medical facilities and airfare cost money, so do skilled workers and staff. It takes money.

Money isn't anything but a way of standardizing the value of things, so we can exchange them. Back in earlier times, I might have made shoes, and you might have sold pots. Maybe we agreed that two shoes equaled one pot. Says who? We did. In the next town, maybe the shoemaker wanted two pots for a pair of shoes. Later on, money was created to set a standard, so if two shoes equaled a dollar and one pot equaled a dollar, everyone knew that two shoes cost the same as one pot. With money, if you didn't want a pot, but wanted to get food or clothes, you had a system that set the relative values of items so that you could get whatever you wanted.

Money is only a tool. It's nothing to love or focus your goals on all by itself. Money can be used for good works or evil deeds. It can be invested and work for you, or you can work for it all your life and waste what you get on selfish junk. What will you use your fortune for?

In the same way, becoming famous is nothing to work toward. People will put the most personal parts of their lives on television shows today, and for what? For 15 minutes of fame? Stupid stuff gets put up on YouTube—and for what? To get in the spotlight, maybe get picked up in some viral e-mail and have millions see you make a fool of yourself? I see kids trying to look like thugs and gangstas, playing the part, hoping someone notices. Craving attention and fame causes people to do crazy things.

And once they've got it, what happens? People get all outrageous and act even more crazy and irresponsible. My daughter and son see this kind of stuff, and so do millions of other kids. Like any kind of success, fame brings responsibility, but lots of people in the spotlight don't seem to care about anyone but themselves. Is it any wonder so many spin out and blow it all? We may want to avoid the responsibility for our decisions, but we will always bear the consequences—good or bad.

In the movie *Scarface*, Al Pacino ends up alone, paranoid, stuck in his penthouse, and stuck with the drugs that made him rich. He had all the trappings of a rich and successful life, but they didn't bring him happiness. Drugs bought the lifestyle, but not the life. They brought him the bitter consequences of anger, resentment, fear, emptiness, and ultimately death.

When the average person looks at someone like me, who has achieved a certain level of success, it's easy to imagine all the material things that wealth brings. Nice cars, big houses, fancy vacations at five-star resorts—these are the sugarplums filling the heads of those who are outside looking in. I can tell you that it's nice to live comfortably and not worry about how expensive the restaurant tab may be, but I'll let you in on a little secret: it's not the material things that make your life fulfilling and satisfying. If that's all you have going for you, I can guarantee you will *never* be happy. You need to have other dimensions to your life, things that can't be added up in dollars and cents.

Money and Fame Alone Are Empty Dreams

It's been said fame is fleeting . . . and it sure is. Fame and fortune alone is selfish, it's all about *me*. There's a whole lot bigger legacy you can leave behind. You can touch other people's lives and change the world.

Somewhere along the way people started chasing fame and fortune. Money itself, remember, isn't good or evil, but the love of it is. That evil will eat you from the inside out, just as surely as success will grow you from the inside out.

Even people who are super successful go through a kind of passage at some point of mental or spiritual value adjustments. What comes out at the other end are two separate groups:

1. Those who are basically unhappy, untrusting, miserly types; takers, not givers.
2. Those who realize that true success involves a mind-change toward an attitude of giving back, not just getting.

And I believe that by embracing a giving mindset sooner, rather than later, we can achieve success sooner as well. In fact, I've proven it in my own life. Here are a few examples of financially super successful individuals who figured this out, and you probably know a whole lot more:

- *Andrew Carnegie* piled away a ton of money. The mogul of U.S. Steel epitomized the image of the robber baron. Yet, the Carnegie Foundation that he set up with a $1.5 million gift in 1903 funded 2,509 public and university libraries—at a time when most towns, even most cities, had none. He changed America. He gave back. He became known as the "Patron Saint of Libraries."

- *John H. Johnson*, publisher of the breakthrough magazine *Ebony*, the first black publication to reach a national market with national advertisers, became the first African American on the Forbes 400 list of richest Americans. Because of his commitments to education and philanthropy, his company's Ebony Fashion Show has raised more than $50 million for charity since its founding in 1958.

- The *Ford Foundation* was founded in 1936 by *Henry* and *Edsel Ford* to "Strengthen democratic values, reduce poverty and injustice, promote international cooperation and advance human achievement." With over $11 billion in assets and $572 million spent on programs in 2005, Ford today is the second largest charitable foundation in the world.

- *Annie Minerva Turnbo Malone* became known as America's "First Black Millionairess" in the 1920s (even though Madam C. J. Walker is listed in *Guinness* as the first self-made woman millionaire in America). Malone trained over 75,000 sales agents for careers in sales of her company's hair care products. At one time, she was reported to have been supporting two full-time students in every black land grant college in the nation. She was a huge supporter of historically black colleges and universities around the country, and even founded one herself: Poro College. She also funded the building of the St. Louis Colored Orphans Home, which was later renamed the Annie Malone Children's Home in her honor.

- More recently, *Bill Gates*, arguably the world's richest man, established the Bill and Melinda Gates Foundation. His goals include equipping every public library with Internet access, funding global health initiatives for vaccines (especially, for malaria) and population control programs, and creating the largest private college scholarship program in history. He kicked his foundation off with (get this) $17 billion dollars— and has so far committed over 60 percent of his wealth (his goal is 95 percent), making it the world's largest philanthropic organization.

- In 2006, *Warren Buffett*, head of Berkshire Hathaway and arguably the world's most savvy investor gave the bulk of his fortune to the Gates Foundation. His $30.7 billion gift doubled the size of the Gates Foundation to $60 billion, over five times the assets of the Ford Foundation. Who will start the next number one charitable organization?

- When *Bill Cosby's* son Ennis died, Bill and his wife Camille started a foundation in his name to assist at-risk and financially strapped, often urban, schools. They've provided almost a million books to nearly 8,000 under-resourced classrooms in over 500 cities since 2000.

- *Oprah Winfrey* has contributed more than $40 million toward the creation of the Oprah Winfrey Leadership Academy Foundation. Oprah's Angel Network has raised more than $50 million to help establish scholarships and schools, support women's shelters, and build youth centers and homes—changing the future for people all over the world.

Slate.com lists an annual "Slate 60" philanthropy list—which in 2005 topped $4.3 billion in various donations by wealthy, super-successful businesspeople—and estimates that over $250 billion was given by all Americans that year. Why did these incredibly rich and successful people give so much away? They'd already built their fortune, dynasties of business and wealth. If you ask them why, the answer is universally the same: ***the desire to give back, to leave a legacy.*** Making big bucks is a game that stops being fun and stops having any meaning all by itself, and super-successful people all reach a point where they ask, "Is that all there is . . . ?"

So What's the Point?

It's easy to point to wealthy people and say "Sure, they've got lots of dough. They *should* be giving it away. In fact, tell them to send some my way!" But I didn't wait until I was a millionaire to pursue my own altruistic plans. For example, I worked with my father's church, helping the congregation learn about stewardship and giving, and helped the church invest their funds wisely. This led directly to business models we use in our companies today. You see, giving doesn't cost you; it blesses you. That's why the Bible says if you "Cast your bread on the water, it will come back after many days."

I went to Gambia and Senegal as part of a mission to deliver medical supplies. I was there for two weeks and did some computer work for their department of education. I even went through the "rites of passage" out in the bush and was given the name *Amoro*. I've taught classes at church and at Boys and Girls Clubs, stepped in and taught the entrepreneurship class at my wife's old high school, Paseo Academy, a high school in Kansas City, Missouri, and volunteered at my church.

There have been studies that show nearly 75 percent of the giving done in the United States is by individuals and families—regular people, not wealthy benefactors. When most people think of a philanthropist, they imagine some old, rich white male. In the African American community, the culture of giving goes way back. Those who got out of slavery often would save for years to buy other family members out of slavery.

Millions of former slaves, along with many caring white philanthropists, largely funded the growth of black land grant colleges in the late 1800s. They supported their churches and loaned each other the little money they had to start businesses after the Civil War. Even today, African Americans give more than any other group, up to 25 percent more of their discretionary income than white Americans according to the *Chronicle of Philanthropy*. Black households average $1,614 in donations to their favorite causes. Of course, the black church is a key partner in all this, and many black families tithe (give 10 percent of their income) or more to their local church.

Remember Oseola McCarty? She wasn't some mogul of industry. She took in other people's laundry (and they had to drop it off at her house because she didn't even own a car). Yet, she left $150,000 to the University of Southern Mississippi to provide scholarships for minority students leaving a legacy that will keep changing lives for years to come.

Nowadays we see Mexican and Central Americans working hard, often for jobs that here in the United States most citizens deem beneath them. They live with 10 people in a house and endure all sorts of hardships, prejudice, and low pay, sending the bulk of their money back home to support families they've been separated from, sometimes for years.

The concept of giving back is part of what makes us human and connects us. The miser's heart is a heart of greed, one that is alone, and he will die with no legacy, no one to notice he is gone, and no one to care. Be a giver, not a taker, and you'll find true success much more quickly.

Giving Is the True Success

True success comes when we use our abilities to improve the lives of people around us. True success comes when we learn the principles behind these kinds of actions, and guess what? We can start applying these powerful success principles without having a dime in the bank.

The giving mindset doesn't always have to be tied to money. Even if you don't have a lot of money, you can give your time. Go to a homeless shelter and serve food. Go to a retirement home and just walk around, smile, and talk with the people. Tutor a child. Be a Big Brother or Big Sister. Take some food to someone that's homebound. Give of yourself.

Creating a Habit of Giving Is the Shortcut to True Success

When we give, we put ourselves out there, on the line. And guess what? A lot of people begin to respond with cooperation and assistance to help us grow successfully. I believe, and I have proven, that success can come faster to those who learn to be givers early, instead of takers.

Money for money's sake . . . you can have it. But making money so we can improve the world around us, that's where it's at. It's the best part of having plenty. Just think of the happiness you feel when you give a young kid a great birthday present. Now expand that to the happiness you would feel if you could buy your parents a new house. Let's go even higher—think of the joy you'd get from giving an entire underprivileged neighborhood a new school so that generations can be blessed by your gift. You can't lose when you're a giver. When you give someone else a great deal of happiness and joy, it comes right back to you.

I Don't Do It for Money, Neither Should You!

I'm a big believer in having goals that are bigger than myself, that can't be achieved in just one lifetime. Making money just can't be the end of it all. I mean, if making money was Bill Gates' only goal or dream, do you really think he'd keep working? He's in the number one seat when it comes to money. He's made almost a *billion* dollars for every year he's been alive ($46.6 billion).

Gates had a dream to change the whole way we use computers. To take computers out of the deep-freeze rooms of the old mainframes and put them on the desktops of every office, school, and home in America. Are we there yet? No, but computers are in over 60 percent of U.S. homes, and that's saying a lot for a geeky guy who started with a clunky program. He loves his work! He loves the creativity, the ideas, the engineering and problem solving, the deal making, and the visionary stuff. He loves it all.

And now, as I've already mentioned, the richest man has created the world's wealthiest charity, the Bill and Melinda Gates Foundation. He's just as driven to work long hours to realize this dream, this passion, as he was to build Microsoft. I guarantee you, he doesn't consider it work. His vision is bigger than his life, and it will keep on after he's long gone.

I believe in this dimension of success very strongly. It goes even deeper than the joy of doing work you are passionate about and love. It is the joy of *creating a greater good*. By this, I mean looking beyond yourself, your needs and wants, to something bigger, something that makes a difference in the world: a new inner-city preschool, a new church building, an ongoing scholarship for underprivileged students, or planting trees in barren, urban parks. To be able to look back and say to yourself, "I made that happen!" That for me is the prize in the Cracker Jack box, the cherry on the sundae, and the pot of gold at the end of the rainbow.

Why do you think all those super successful people I listed earlier decided to give away so much of their fortunes? Because real success is when you can comfortably share what you have in a significant way. Just that simple act of giving gives me a better feeling than all the honors and accolades I've been given. Having money for more than just more stuff. Using money to change lives . . . *that's true success.*

> We need to dream big dreams, propose grandiose means if we are to recapture the excitement, the vibrancy, and pride we once had.
>
> —*Coleman Young*

You don't have to wait to start changing the world around you, no more than you have to wait for anything else. No matter where you are at in your life and career, you can touch other people's lives right now. The opportunities are all around you. Touching even one life makes a difference. Do it now.

Socially-Conscious Investing

There's just no excuse for not giving back, no matter where you are or how much you make, or don't make. But for me, taking it from a personal level to a corporate level is where I always saw these giving concepts get bogged down. That's why, from the earliest days of our company, I decided that a large portion of our efforts would be aimed at giving back: building up and empowering people in local communities. As a result, I've sought out projects that are not only good business ventures, but are also programs that create and strengthen individuals and communities here in America and overseas.

Often it's just been an idea shared by a small group of people and myself. Then the idea becomes plans and drawings. Then we begin presenting this great idea to investors around the country, and some get excited and get involved. Credit-Investors line up to buy the new and rehabbed houses, allowing us to create more. It turns into bricks and mortar, houses and buildings. People will raise families in those houses and earn their living in those shops. It's hard to describe the sense of fulfillment and excitement that I get from watching this entire process take place.

I see people struggling to buy gas for their cars so they can get to work. Elderly people struggling to have heating oil for their homes. Cities wasting millions on oil and gas, when less expensive solutions would mean more for social services. With Goshen's biofuels initiatives, we're able to address these issues as well as be environmentally sound, create jobs, and give assistance to subsistence farmers.

You know how all this makes me feel at the end of the day? Fantastic! That's why I encourage anyone who seeks to achieve any kind of success to **dream big dreams.** The simple truth is that if you feel good doing work that you love, you'll feel even better doing things that enhance and uplift the world around you.

True success really is about giving back.

You might think this statement is hopelessly corny. But when people ask me about my equation for success, I have to say that giving back is the greatest factor. And, as I pointed out before, you don't have to have a dime to begin using this success principle right now.

John Wesley, who with his brother Charles defied king and country to begin the Methodist church, said it this way:

Do all the good you can.

By all the means you can.

In all the ways you can.

In all the places you can.

To all the people you can.

As long as ever you can.

I can't say it any better than that.

SECTION VI

Getting What You Need to Succeed

How's Your Starter Switch?

Have you ever wondered what the biggest difference is between entrepreneurs and everybody else? I'd say it is their ability to be self-starters. They have drive and they have initiative. They don't need their momma, their teacher, or some boss to tell them to get up and do what needs to be done. They aren't passive people; they are active. In fact, they are *pro*-active, taking action *before* they have to, instead of reacting after the fact. Entrepreneurs are the ones who get everybody else moving.

With me, it was just a matter of having an idea and following it up. "You want a video game? Go figure out how to make one yourself." See, most people—kids or adults—would have just put on an attitude and gotten angry, like the world owed them that game or something. Some might have even decided to lift one from a store, or from some other kid . . . get it any way they could, just because they wanted it, like that made it right.

But for me, that idea was the beginning of everything. That was my starter switch. It became a dream, a vision that took on a life of its own. It would get me excited and motivated because I could envision the outcome. After that, it was just a matter of doing the steps that needed to be done to make that idea come true.

At first, it just meant going to the library and reading a few books. Then I needed to work some odd jobs, so I could buy some books of my own. Friends told me I was crazy when I didn't make it to a party or down to the skating rink, but I didn't care. I had this dream going on in my head, and I knew it was real . . . I just needed to get it out.

> A dream doesn't become reality through magic; it takes sweat, determination, and hard work.
>
> —*Colin Powell*

There were times it meant staying up all night trying to figure out technical manuals (remember, I was still in school). I didn't care, though, because it was my thing, my dream. I think I could've worked 24 hours a day if I had to, to get it happening. I started asking around to find people who could explain parts I didn't understand. Eventually my dream even meant borrowing money for my business. For me and other entrepreneurs, there is an inner fire that keeps us moving forward.

One day I came across a *Forbes* magazine list of the wealthiest people around, and that became part of my goal. I've been working toward it ever since. I mean, I knew I could have the lifestyle, but even more important, I knew I would reach a point where I didn't have to work for the money anymore and could do things like medical and educational missions and things like that. Working a job wouldn't get that for me, not the way I wanted it.

What never occurred to me during all this time were all the reasons I *couldn't* do something—like I was too young or I was black or nobody had done this before or it might not succeed. Those thoughts were never a part of my mindset. I guess I was just blind to those things. I could see it all just like it was real. I already knew where I was heading, and I was making it happen. I didn't have time to focus on all the negatives.

When I taught an entrepreneur class at Paseo Academy, I explained to my students why knowledge alone is not power, and why only applied knowledge gives you real power. I still tell teenagers and college students to take what they already know how to do, and simply apply it, *right now*.

What makes someone think they'll start applying knowledge on some magic day in the future, when we don't use what we already have? Sort of like Mardi Gras, Mardi Gras, Mardi Gras. Party, party, party. Then suddenly it all changes at midnight from Fat Tuesday to Ash Wednesday, and we start dealing with real life decisions. That's not a plan. That's not even a hope-for. That's some kind of fantasy.

Whatever you want to do, go ahead and start small, but start. Start today. Figure out a way to apply what you already know, and get the additional knowledge you need to take it further as you go along.

I don't see any programs out there instilling these concepts in our kids, that these things are accomplishable *right now*, in the present—especially among urban youth. I have seen some local volunteer programs, usually underfunded, trying to change this. But on a national basis, it's still the same old "Go to school, go to college, get buried under all those student loans, all the student debt. *Then* get a 'good job,' work 30 years, and then retire." I just don't see this approach working anymore in our society, if it ever really did for most graduates.

Teaching the Characteristics of Success

What if instead, we taught students in high school to be self-sufficient, to be self-starters and entrepreneurs. So even if they don't own their own company they can have the kinds of skills that make them valuable employees for somebody else? In fact, why not start in elementary school . . . before they have time to learn all the things you "can't" do?

When Cheyney University approached me in 2006 to establish an Entrepreneurship Academy, I jumped at the chance. Cheyney is the oldest historically black college or university in the United States. I'm working with them to develop interactive entrepreneurial programs for young people. Cheyney is creating the Ephren W. Taylor II Entrepreneurship Academy, specifically to get the kind of information that's in this book into the hands of young people.

But I challenged them. I said, "If you're going to have an entrepreneurship program, then make it a real-world, hands-on entrepreneurship program." I mean, why have students sitting around in a classroom instead of going out and actually talking to somebody who runs a real company? You want to learn about human resource issues? Find somebody who actually deals with serious human resource issues every day first, at a real company, and then you can relate to why you need to know what's inside some book.

Show me how the accounting principles I'm studying will help me know how to buy a company. Help me understand how those composition courses I took will help me craft a business plan, a proposal, a prospectus. Show me how this training will help me get funding, help me run my business.

I believe we need to look at our current curriculums and redesign some of these classes to start teaching using real world experience, versus just playing around with dead facts from books. If we do this right, the students could go a lot further, and a lot more would stay in the loop. They could see the connection, the application of their training and education. I encourage you to visit www.EphrenUniversity .com for more about the Entrepreneurship Academy and the hands-on teaching programs we're making available.

This is essentially what happened to me when I interned with a mentor and ran my own businesses while I was in school. For me, my "college" was doing intense self-study work, asking questions, making contacts, and finding mentors. I took specialized training classes like those at the Kauffmann Foundation entrepreneurship program, and others sponsored by the Future Business Leaders of America, where I led a team of aspiring business leaders to state, then national championships. College for me was the crucible of my own real-world business, which I built to a national company employing a bunch of people including my high-school history teacher.

I was always a self-starter. I didn't need anyone telling me when it was okay. I didn't bypass my education at all, I just went after it differently. But I did go for it, because I was focused on my goal.

Our Dreams Are the Power behind Our Motivation

The real question is, how much of a self-starter are you? What are your passions? Have you ever decided to learn a new skill and then gone out and done it on your own? Have you ever started exercising or have you lost weight by creating your own program and following it religiously?

Maybe you had an idea about creating or building something from scratch and you didn't stop until it was done. These are the kinds of things entrepreneurs do. We don't even give it a second thought. It's just the way our brains work. Part of it is that ability to visualize the end result, hold it in your mind and keep moving toward your goal. When setbacks come, you don't let them beat you down. Just pick up and start over again. Just keep navigating your life in that direction and you will reach your goal.

I am not discouraged because every wrong attempt discarded is another step forward.

—*Thomas A. Edison*

If this describes you, it might be time for you to break the mold and get out on your own. You are not a slave—you really are free. Your thoughts and your feelings are yours. Your dreams, your goals, and ultimately your actions and attitudes are entirely yours to do with as you wish. You are the boss over these areas. Now what are you going to do with that power?

You're free to be negative and destructive, to go for the bling and forget everyone else. You're free to be selfish and uncaring if that's all that you want in your life.

You're also free to be positive and creative, to go for success and take as many people along with you as possible. You are free to use your success as a platform to help even more people—free to change lives, change neighborhoods, and change the world. Even though parts of your life may be controlled by other people, you can start being your own boss in those areas you *do* have control over, and begin experiencing the freedom of doing your own thing. I can tell you firsthand, there is no satisfaction like the satisfaction you get from creating a business or a product from scratch and watching it succeed. And then being free to enjoy that success and use it to help others.

Where to Get the Information and Knowledge You Need

A common excuse I talked about in an earlier section is "How can I start a business when I don't know anything about _____?" Fill in the blank. The blank could be running a barber shop, starting a cab company, or becoming a stock broker. It could be buying an oil well, building airplanes, driving a truck, or whatever your dream is.

Even if your goal is not a business, when we start out we are all empty slates, with none of the knowledge or real-world experience we need to succeed. I never said you didn't need to have the knowledge, or at least know where to get the knowledge, in order to succeed. Using knowledge as an excuse is an entirely different thing from recognizing the need to have certain specialized knowledge, and going and getting it.

Even worse than starting out with nothing, more often than not we start out full of junk—bad habits and misinformation. Whether you're talking relationships or business, we have to flush out the bad before we can grow. We have to "unlearn" what we've been taught about life, business, our potential, and "conventional wisdom."

There Are No Excuses for Failure

Assuming you know how to read, write, and speak the English language with a relatively useable degree of skill, excuses like "I don't know" or "I don't have anything" are pretty weak. In my mind, there's just no excuse for lacking the information and knowledge you need to succeed today. It's too available, too accessible, and most of it's free for the taking.

Remember it was a *Forbes* magazine that really got my juices going, talking about the wealthiest people in the world. But put *Forbes* magazines into most high school libraries? Forget it. They've got *Vibe*, *Jet*, *Cosmo*, and all sorts of flashy, gossipy, society, sports and entertainment publications, but no real information that kids might accidentally discover that could change their lives. It doesn't matter. Plan on taking it on yourself to go out and find information.

Even without all the online information that's yours for the taking, there are literally millions of books available. They may not all be at your public library but they're somewhere. Once you decide what you want to do, you can read, study, and teach yourself what you need to know. You don't have to sit in a classroom and wait for a teacher to teach it to you.

I had a good foundation to start from because my mother taught us so much at home before we even entered school. Before I even went to first grade, Mom had taught me, and later my brothers, to read and write our names both in cursive and in print. So I had a big head start over other kids who were struggling to learn these skills from scratch.

My mom taught me something that is so obvious you might groan when you read it but for me it was the key to the treasury:

> *Everything you need to know is in*
> *a book somewhere.*

Much of my education came from reading books. I taught myself how to program computers. I taught myself how to write business plans. I taught myself how to find capital and read annual reports. I read everything an MBA student would have to, and worked out all the examples they gave, just like I was in a class with a teacher looking over my shoulder. Just about everything I know was self-taught.

The things I didn't learn on my own I learned from mentors. When I got up into the bigger business circles, it was easy for those guys to take me on and pour their knowledge into me. I could keep up because I'd done my homework before we ever met. They brought me up to speed on the lingo and the acronyms and all the stuff about financing and shares and stock, about 10-Qs and 8-Ks, pink sheets and institutional money. By then I had enough background and basic knowledge to keep up so I could take their information and run with it even further.

I don't think I'm the smartest guy in the world, I'm just one of the most resourceful. What that means is that I don't need a teacher or a classroom if I really want to learn. I can go get it myself, whatever I need, wherever and whenever I need it. Can you see how empowering this one simple step can be? I'm not dependent on whatever the "system" chooses to teach me. I have the ability to go out and get what I need, on my own. Or I know how to find someone who's already been there and done the things I want to do and have them teach me.

Mentors

Without mentors, we have no examples to follow for our major decisions in life. In business, I consider this suicidal. It's easy to find a mentor if you're serious about getting one. I have been fortunate to have some incredible mentors in my life. But I take the approach that everyone on my team should be "mentor quality" as well.

This is one of the main reasons I have surrounded myself with quality, high-performance experts, people I can turn to who have the experience to give me the answers I need. They know when I am focused on a project, I don't listen to the "cannot be done" mantra. I want the "here's how we can do it" solutions. I make sure they also have a vested interest in the success of our development projects. In fact, my team of professionals personally invest in our projects, so they share any risk of the investments along with our clients and shareholders. I look to this team to provide me with the kind of key information I need to make quality decisions. And I listen. And then I make the final decisions based on what they've told me, and what I know—and feel—is the right way to go.

Sometimes I find them, sometimes they find me. I found Emerson Brantley online. I had several people handle marketing at different times in my companies. I wasn't real happy with the results I was getting. Some cost me plenty and still didn't bring me the results I wanted. Then, as I often do, I went online and started scoping out marketing people, specifically direct-response marketing. That's the kind we used the most: targeted mail and other campaigns to specific kinds of prospective investors. For a small business, trying to do expensive broadcast and other mass marketing is a waste of money. It is far better to figure out exactly who your real market is, and the best ways to reach them and only them. This way, you're not wasting your message on thousands of people who don't care and aren't interested. They're not your market.

I found Emerson, read over the information on his site, and saw his experience was exactly what I was looking for. He'd done thousands of campaigns, for all kinds of companies, but especially in real estate and investing. So I e-mailed him, and let him know I'd like to retain him over the next 18 months. Before we ever talked.

How did I know to hire him? I trusted my instincts. I saw the results he could get me way ahead of time, and he made them become a reality in more ways than one. Much more than just with the marketing, which alone was way beyond anything I even imagined. He also saw my vision of socially conscious investing, and didn't just run with it, he added to it. He enhanced it with his knowledge and experience. He saw the potential of the company, and magnified it. Instead of telling me what I couldn't do, or shouldn't attempt, he bumped up the ante big time. Quantum leap he called it, and that's what he believed. It was a natural leap for me, and I believed it, and saw it as already accomplished. All that was left was to make it happen, which we did—which we continue to do.

Sometimes people find me, like Harvey Lynch did. He went looking for someone like me, and there I was. He wanted a young African American CEO to share his wealth of knowledge and experience in oil and gas and natural energy. He has enhanced our company and taken us into whole new areas I would have never considered before. Like many of my team, he's a mentor as well. It's because of Harvey that City Capital is moving into the renewable energy fields and establishing ourselves as players in this wide-open field. Biofuels give us the chance to be a catalyst for socially-conscious investing that benefits communities as well as being environmentally conscious for our planet.

Melissa and Treavor Grimes found me in a different way. I was speaking on finances at a church in Detroit, Michigan. They had been married a year, and were still adjusting financially to being married. They came with another mentor of mine while they were vacationing in Detroit (for their first anniversary),to learn new ways to deal with the financial issues in their life. We had a larger crowd than expected, and they volunteered to help out. We always sit down right after an event to discuss things we did right, and things that need to be improved, and I asked them to hang around and join us.

Melissa was honest and direct, and had some solid critiques and suggestions. I asked her if she'd be willing to volunteer some, to help us out. She agreed, but after a few months of this it got to be too much. She was pregnant, and spending more hours volunteering for me than working her regular job.

I already knew I wanted her on the team, so I made her an offer to come aboard. Melissa helped me start our new corporate office in Franklin, Tennessee, first in my home and later at our current location. When the time came in our company for a chief operations officer, Melissa was the clear choice in my mind. And she's tough. Emerson calls her the glue that holds the team together, and she is.

"Ephren tells me I'm harder on him than most people are," says Melissa. "But it's because with great vision there has to be some balance. I'm sort of the detail person, the one on the ground. He knows how to get off ground zero and get that 40,000 foot vision . . . and then make the hard decisions to move our company forward. He's a lot more comfortable taking those risks than I would be, but I pull the pieces together and get the team in action so we can make it happen."

Melissa and Treavor are both active in City Capital and my other projects now. Treavor heads up an entertainment division of mine, working with performers and promoting worthy productions around the country.

Looking for the Win-Win

Sometimes my team has found me, like Melissa or Harvey, and sometimes I've found them, like with Emerson. The way I've brought together most of my support team, though, is by us finding each other. What I mean is, when you're going about the business of doing business, when you're out there doing all the things we've talked about, you meet people. And they know other people and you meet them, and on and on. You can call it networking if you want, but what matters isn't how many business cards you collect. Like everything else, what matters is what you do with the quality contacts you meet.

I look for the ways that we might be able to mesh the things we do. Ways they can help me achieve my goals, and ways I can reciprocate so it's always a win-win deal. I start out from the beginning respecting them, and looking for ways we can help each other. I'm not looking for one-way relationships, all taking and no giving. If you're a taker, all you gain will be taken from you sooner or later. Don't be a taker, don't be a hater. Be a giver. You know, the Golden Rule:

Do unto others as you would have others do unto you.

—*Matthew 7:12*

At least 21 of the major world religions have this same principle, which some refer to as the Rule of Reciprocity. Sometimes this is negatively stated as, "What goes around, comes around." In every case, the lesson is that like a rubber ball thrown against a wall, whatever we give out comes back to us. Be a hater, get hated. Be a taker, plan on losing out in the end. Be a giver, and it'll be given to you again and again. I believe what we should give out should be good for others.

In all of the ways my people run our business, we approach every opportunity as givers, not takers. This is especially true when we're working with governmental officials. We ask what we can do to help them achieve what they want for their people—their community, their

---

This old guy was sitting on his front porch, watching the water rise and praying, "Lord, I put all my trust in you. I believe you'll save me if it's Your will." (You've heard that one before.)

One of his neighbors came driving his 4 × 4 through the rising water, and the neighbor yelled at him, "Hop in, this water's rising fast," but the old man said, "God will look after me. He'll provide."

As the water started coming up on the porch, the old man headed inside just as the rescue workers came by and called to him from a boat. "Jump in the boat so we can get you to high land." But he said, "No, I've got faith everything will be alright. God will save me."

Finally, he got on the roof and a helicopter came by, dropping a ladder. But he waved them off and said, "My God is sufficient. He'll take care of me."

The helicopter flew off, the water washed the man away and he drowned. When he woke up in heaven he asked God, "Why didn't you save me? Wasn't my faith strong enough?" See, right away he blamed God.

And God said, "I sent your neighbor, I sent the rescue workers, I even sent a helicopter crew, but you wouldn't budge."

Too often we all want the miracle, the easy fix, the lottery ticket to success. But most of the time, God uses everyday people to do His will.

state, their country. Many have never been approached this way before, and the results are phenomenal. Our win-win approach allows us to structure deals that others simply cannot believe.

So in the same way, when you make a new contact, realize that he or she has value, first as a human being, but perhaps also to help you reach your goal. Approach the relationship openly and positively, and try to find the ways you can benefit the contact as well. When we don't, we shut down many of the opportunities before we even know they exist.

How often do we meet people that could help us get to our dream, depending on our positive, or negative attitude and response to them? How many times have we passed up opportunities in our lives that could have made all the difference in our own success, simply because of bad thinking or inaction on our part? It reminds me of the story I once heard about a man who was stuck in a flood.

I've found an amazing number of contacts over the years, "everyday people" more than willing to open the doors and help me succeed, *when I've been open to the opportunity*. When I'm thinking like a giver, not a taker. Trusting myself and being willing to listen. Not so much worried about "What do they want from me?" or "What's in it for me?" (one of Emerson's favorite marketing expressions), but more interested in "How can I make this a win-win relationship?"

The Mentors around Us

You may have a mentor in your life already but you may not have taken the time to mine the treasury of knowledge they hold. Your favorite teacher or coach can be a mentor. Even an older sister or brother, or uncle or aunt. You may find an author who inspires you. I've found mentors in my church, and I don't mean just the pastors. I mean youth leaders and Sunday School teachers, and elderly people who took time to share their life knowledge with me. Most younger people don't have time for older folks, but that's where all the experience is. Even as a teenager, I figured their experience would save years off my career path to success. And it has.

At 16, How Much Real-World Experience Do You Really Have?

I learned a lot from some of my teachers and coaches. I'm not saying all teachers are saints. Just because a teacher isn't interested in taking extra time with you doesn't mean you shouldn't seek out others who will. Some are just burnt-out from working with mouthy kids all day. Would you want to put in 7 or 8 hours a day dealing with lazy attitudes, rudeness, and disruptive behavior; then go home and put in another 2 or 3 hours grading papers? After all, the kids don't care, the administration doesn't appreciate you, and school boards figure you can live on poverty level because you're "just a teacher?"

So why would a teacher be your mentor? Because every teacher and coach wants to find someone with a real thirst for what they offer, someone who really wants to learn. They want to make a difference . . . you *know* they're not in it for the money. They're just waiting for someone worthy of their efforts and their commitment. They want to believe in you, they're waiting to find that special someone who says, "I want it," so they can say, "I can help you."

Are you going to be that person? That special someone who makes it, who finds the mentors to help them along the way and gets what they need? Or are you going to be the undisciplined player? The one who slacks off in practice, gets in fights, and causes disruptions all the time? Are you going be the one that's not doing your homework, that's not really applying themselves in school? Are you going to be the one with the attitude?

Do You Deserve a Mentor?

It's not up to your mentor to figure out if you're worth it or not. *You've* got to figure it out first for yourself, and then present yourself in a way that says, "I want more of what you know." They don't want another problem to deal with . . . they want someone that listens and applies, someone who's easy to manage in their already limited schedule. You can't just be a wild child wanting, wanting, wanting.

There are very few kids who ever take advantage of this, and usually the other kids pick on them and call them "Teacher's Pet" or brownnose or worse. The question you have to answer for yourself is: Am I going to do something with my life and am I willing to take the necessary steps to cause that change? Or am I going to listen to the losers and give up the opportunity to learn from someone who can shave years off my efforts?

My wife MeShelle always said, "A closed mouth doesn't get fed." So, if you want to find a mentor but you're too scared to ask one to help you, well, you might be surprised the first time you show your interest and speak up. They just might take you up on it, and that's the beginning of a wild ride.

I can just hear you saying, "But Ephren, my whole life's about the streets. I've got more experience about life than most grownups."

Well, maybe you know something about surviving on the street, and maybe you don't know as much of that as you think you do. *We don't know what we don't know.* If we don't even know the right questions to ask, how will we get the answers we need to guide us? So many kids and teens are lost, struggling, and angry. Whenever they get a little money, they blow it on the outward stuff like shoes and cars, bling, flash, junk. But nobody's telling them, "Hey, you might want to think about investing that money. You may want to put it here, or put it there. Watch it grow." When I do an example of this for my entrepreneurship classes, I calculate just how much they could make with the $150 they're blowing every month on partying and junk:

If you'd invest $150 a month, figuring 10 percent interest, you'd be worth almost a million dollars in 40 years ($968,528.05).

Now let's say you had an insurance settlement or an uncle dies or something, and you manage to put together a one-time deposit of $1,000 to open your account. You still only put away $150 a month religiously, but now you'd be up over a million bucks in 40 years: $1,014,910.71.

That's a $46,382.66 difference, just by putting a $1,000 in one time. Then I go into the whole *"Time Value of Money"* thing and their eyes roll back in their heads. I mean, when I share stuff like this with my classes, they say, "Hey, how come nobody ever told us that before?"

See, for most people it's not that they won't listen or gravitate to it. It's just that nobody's been telling them, or telling them in a way people can relate to. And that's the biggest problem I have with the educational system today. It's not that the kids don't have the ability or aptitude. It's not that kids or teenagers aren't not old enough or smart enough to grasp these concepts. It's the simple fact that nobody is putting the information in front of them. And even when they do manage to get the information, we make it really difficult for them to find ways to apply in the real world. That's why it's so important to seek out mentors, and cultivate the relationships that will help give you the winning edge.

Why Not Talk to Someone Who's Been There and Done That?

The reason the Kansas City Missouri School District asked me to teach the class on entrepreneurism in the first place was *because I was not a teacher*. I was somebody who's actually out in the business world and successful at what I do. And I was real young, very close to the age of the kids in the class, so they could relate to me. High school students, even elementary students, still relate to me because they still see me as not that far ahead of where they are.

The students I talked with got a real feel for what it was like in my world and what it takes to succeed. Unfortunately, that was just one class in one school for one semester. Now I'm working with other school districts and have been invited to teach these concepts to college-level business classes, churches, Boys & Girls Clubs, and other venues all over America. The Ephren W. Taylor II Entrepreneurship Academy at Cheyney University will fine-tune this message and these concepts. At Cheyney, we plan on giving practical real-world, hands-on experience to the students, expose them to mentors, and provide internship opportunities so they can apply everything they are taught in their classes. Most students never have a real entrepreneur come and talk to their class, much less teach a class for an entire semester. But there's no reason for you to wait for that to happen to take and use the information you have right here in your own life. At www.Ephren University.com, students can take online classes on entrepreneurship and find even more resources to help them grow. And you can always go out and find a mentor and make it happen for yourself.

Akeela

In the movie *Akeelah and the Bee*, a young girl from south Los Angeles, Akeelah, played by Keke Palmer, finds out she's got a talent for spelling. Her principal and teacher encourage her so she enters and wins several local spelling bees. Along the way, her best friend gets mad and deserts her, her brother basically tells her she's "acting white," and even her mother gets upset because she has got more important things to do, and no money for extras, like bus fare to get Akeelah to spelling practice. The whole community essentially tells her that education and intelligence are for other people. The message they send is that she needs to learn who she is and stop trying to be something she isn't. She has to overcome these crippling messages from her family and her community, as well as her own feelings of inadequacy, just to get up and even try to compete.

So what does she do? *She turns from them to another*. Akeelah hooks up with a mentor, Dr Joshua Larabee (Laurence Fishburne). He's a tough character who doesn't take trash or trash talk. He demands excellence, proper language, and manners. I'm here to tell you, mentors—good mentors—will be tough as nails on you. If you think that they're going to be like your grandma and pat your hand and tell you everything's all right, think again.

At one point, all the negative stuff gets so overwhelming and Akeela quits. Gives up to all the peer pressure. But then her best friend repents, and tells her she's *got* to go for the Scripps National Spelling Bee, and Akeela gets herself up again. She goes back to Dr. Larabee and even takes the crosstown bus to an upscale white school for more training. Surprisingly, she finds more acceptance there than at home. Even the top-dog speller respects her (although his father disses her talent).

Ultimately, Akeela makes it to the National Spelling Bee, and in doing so unites her neighborhood. And she wins! Suddenly, she's a hero. Everyone's proud of her. Even the local gang leader asks her to read one of his poems, and he slaps one of his homies when he shoots off his mouth at Akeela, then he tells her she did good for the hood.

I've told you how I was the lone black nerd in my school. I can relate to how isolated Akeelah must have felt. I also understand her drive and determination. I had two supportive parents, but there was this thing inside me that always said, "Hey, I can do that. I'm GONNA do that." And somehow I understood early on that I needed mentors to guide me, coach me, and help me on my way.

Choosing the Right Mentor

You want to go after somebody who's been successful doing what you want to do. Someone who's where you want to be, not someone whose marriage or business is just starting out. Don't go out and grab the guy who's taken a couple of businesses bankrupt, lost three or four houses, and plays the casinos every weekend. And don't go sit at the feet of someone who's messed up his or her marriage big time, either. Get someone who's *"Been there, done that."*

Go after individuals who have done things for themselves and succeeded because their wisdom is something that can be translated directly into your life in a real, positive way. A lot of young people have issues about getting wisdom from the older generation. I mean, what young person goes out and really seeks advice from somebody who's older? Their thinking is usually, "What can *they* show me that applies to today? All they know is old school." Some kids are so dumb they'll trust what other dumb kids teach them before they'll trust an older expert.

An experienced mentor can tell you a lot. Just trust me on this: Ask them. But for so many young people it's like, "We don't want to hear anything that's not what we think is right. We want to make up our own minds, do our own thing."

But what if you actually find someone who cares enough to ask you hard questions, like "Let's see your budget. Can you afford this? How are you going to make ends meet with all those debts?" What if they give you real solid knowledge—the kind that only comes from experience? It's the most powerful thing that you can acquire. It's priceless. It's almost better than instant gratification because *what they know can shave years off your success track, whether in business or in relationships.*

Respect Gains Respect

I've mentioned Torré Reese and his work with at-risk kids in Liemert Park, California. I consider him a real hero and a mentor to hundreds of young men and women. Keith and Karen Johnson of the Los Angeles T-village Project are a couple of other great mentors. Keith is executive director of T-Village, a nonprofit organization dedicated to empowering at-risk youth with the skills necessary to succeed.

They also coach the Southern California Falcons Youth Football Team, which is how we met. The Falcons are part of the Snoop Youth Football League. Keith and Karen also coach the Falcons Cheer & Drumline Youth and "a whole lot more" as Karen says.

I've seen Keith stop practice because one of the guys mouthed off at his sister and called her a "ho." Everything stopped. That day they stood in the hot California sun for over an hour, and learned a lesson about respect. You can't respect yourself if you're disrespectful to others. Period.

When someone disses another person like that, you're seeing their heart and soul. Their inside, it's like it's dead. They don't have any self-respect going on. Oh, they may act tough and strong, but it's all a front. That Hummer or Mercedes? All that bling around their neck? They're just compensating for something.

Confidence and respect go hand in hand. Both are things that some people seem to just have, but I've got to tell you, it doesn't just happen. It comes from somewhere. I mean, confidence and self-respect can be built inside us. I got mine from the way my parents raised us and encouraged us, but it's possible for all of us to have confidence, to have self-respect. If you didn't get it growing up, we'll talk about how you can start working on it now. Keith and Karen teach both to the kids they work with. I met them in the spring of 2006. Here's Keith's version:

> *Ephren Taylor is restoring hope in the older generation, many of whom were on the verge of believing our younger generation was hopeless. I've found him to be unselfish, even selfless with the gifts God has bestowed upon you. This extends beyond the direct financial assistance he has provided urban youth through the Snoop Youth Football League. He freely shares his knowledge and information, giving inspiration and being the identification our young men and women need, to help them more from a point of economic pain and hardship, to economic power.*

Being involved with dedicated people like Keith and Karen, Torré Reese, and others across the country, makes me so aware of the edge I had growing up. My parents built me up; they didn't tear me down. They encouraged my dreams and goals and pumped up my self-respect, self-esteem, and self-confidence. If there's one thing I try to share with

Keith and Karen's kids, as well as young people and young adults all over America, it's that we have to believe in our dreams and build on them. And we need to build each other up, not tear each other down.

Developing a Culture of Excellence, Not One of Failure

Raoul Davis of Ascendant Strategy Group (www.ascendantstrategy. net) manages my speaking engagements around the country. The Urban Wealth Tour is bringing a message of hope and direction into our urban core to reach the kids and families who need a new vision badly. Raoul echoes what Keith wrote:

> *Ephren Taylor represents the potential of our youth. He is a walking example of possibilities. Through him we see that we can turn troubled teens into entrepreneurs; gang leaders into politicians; and dropouts into productive members of society. Ephren has a humble personality, yet he sets an example for boldness. He has tenacity in trying new things and breaking molds, and young people appreciate and can relate to that. By the example of his life, he teaches them that they too can funnel the same energy they may be using to be rebellious, into becoming trailblazers of success.*

And one of the best ways to focus and funnel all that energy and talent in your life is to find a mentor who's done the things you're wanting to do. Chances are, someone else has accomplished similar dreams to yours. Do you think, just for a moment, that someone who had already done what you are dreaming of doing, might just be able to help you reach your dreams?

I can hear your answer, "Sure, Ephren. But they're gonna want something for it . . . everybody has an angle."

You're right. We all have our own agendas because our lives and welfare are our primary concern. But you know what I discovered? Lots of folks are out there, having already accomplished what they set out to do. You know what they want most of all? *To pass on a legacy.* That's their angle. They hope to find someone like you, to share their knowledge and understanding of life and business and faith and all those things.

A worthy mentor doesn't care about making another buck off of you. If you find one that wants to make you pay for their knowledge, they're just another seminar guru in business to make money. That's another way to get the knowledge you need, but it's an expensive one.

Mentors are free. They don't charge for advice, at least I've never been charged by any of my mentors. Did I put in effort, sometimes hours working beside them to learn what they knew? Yes. But none of them every asked me to pull out my wallet for them to share their knowledge. For the most part, mentors get their egos stroked by having a young apprentice, a young Jedi Knight. So, get yourself a mentor, and you've got yourself something of real value—your very own Obi Wan Kenobi.

You have to have your mind in the right place to interact with a mentor and be able to benefit from his or her knowledge this way. You must have an attitude of respect, for yourself and others. If all we care about is how someone looks—their outward appearance, it's easy to figure nobody can teach us or tell us anything. It's like we think, "I'm smart enough, I know enough, why do I need you?" Everyone has value . . . you'd be amazed at the gems you'll pick up along the way if you just ask.

You Don't Know What You Don't Know

Mentors are all over. They're everywhere. I was shopping at one of the big box hardware stores the other day, and met a guy working there who owned a Manhattan apartment. In case you're not from the northeast United States, apartments in Manhattan aren't cheap. He had designed restaurants for a living . . . for a huge national chain. He made half a million bucks a year until his doctor made him quit because of the stress. So now he putters around rehabbing houses, and works 20 hours a week or so to get to talk with other people (and he likes the discount he gets on all his building supplies, too).

What a storehouse of knowledge! He could tell you the logistics of building a restaurant from the ground up . . . how long it would take, what permits were required, how much the equipment would cost, right down to how much different menus will cost the owner in production costs. I was the *only* person who'd even asked him about his experience— actually had a conversation with him—in almost six months since he'd "retired." To everyone else, he was just a handwritten name on an orange shop apron, telling them what aisle the fasteners were on and where to find replacement washers for their sink. What a waste. You know who I'd be calling if I wanted to go into the restaurant business. I guarantee you he'd spill everything he knew about the business if someone came to him and asked him to mentor them.

You think this man's children think of him like this? Like he's some valuable reservoir of experience and knowledge? No way. He's just their Dad. "Yeah, Dad did some kind of stuff with restaurants, worked all over the place. I'm not real sure what it was he did, but I guess he was pretty good." See, they're so familiar with him, they probably never took the time to pick his brains. There are all these people out there with all this knowledge and understanding—and no one asks or even cares. And yet how many of us could use the information they've got stored inside their heads?

All most people see is just some old man or woman—can't be too important. If he was, he sure wouldn't be working here at some dead-end job. Doesn't drive the latest $60,000 car or wear $2,000 suits. I mean, he's selling plumbing supplies, for crying out loud! What can I possibly learn from him? She's some volunteer at the Community Center. I'll never be a loser like that. He's just a greeter at the department store, poor guy. The real losers are the people who pass by these diamond mines of knowledge and information, all because they're not packaged the way people *think* success is supposed to look. Are you starting to see how our mixed-up concepts of what makes someone successful can blind us to people who really are? And so we pass right by them, not realizing the goldmine of information we're passing up.

Would You Recognize Real Success If It Was Right in Front of You?

Sure, Donald Trump or Bill Gates could pull up in VW and start pumping gas in their jeans and a sweatshirt, and we'd know them. Our favorite Hip-Hop or R&B artist could get in line behind us at the Minute Market and we'd know him in an instant. The tabloids love to show the celebs trying to play incognito: "Gotcha. Great disguise." But here's an eye-opening question:

How many of the world's 946 billionaires on the 2007 Forbes *list would you recognize?*

What if they got in a taxicab with you? What if they rolled down the window of some old pickup truck and asked directions? How about if they were picking up their grandkids from the same daycare center your kids were at? Or in a park at their family reunion and invited your kids to play Frisbee? If you were standing on a beach fishing and one of these folks came walking along with their wife, picking up seashells, and asked you how the fishing was? See what I mean?

So when you're out and about, and you meet people, *don't judge the book by its cover*. Take the time to ask people questions about themselves and be prepared to be surprised. Most will have lives and interests and careers you'd never guess in a million years. Will every one be a candidate to be a mentor? Of course not. But you have to start the ball rolling, and not just assume you know how to size up people so well you can separate "winners" from "losers."

I guess part of it's my upbringing. If nothing else, everything starts at home. My parents taught me to read and write, to ask questions, and most of all to respect authority. What's that got to do with mentoring?

Without respect for yourself, you cannot respect others; Without respect for others you cannot have respect for the knowledge others have.

Even if you don't have that kind of environment or background, can you see the sense it all makes? I mean, respect for ourselves starts with respect for others. If we don't value ourselves, we don't tend to put much value on others, and we shut people out. You're going to have to find your way through this. If growing up you were backhanded for asking questions, if it was okay to disrespect people—any people, other kids, and especially adults—you've got to learn a new way. Otherwise just figure you're gonna keep on keepin' on the way you were taught, and shut yourself out from any hope of success. The good news is, you can start a different path today and start finding all sorts of people who'll help you on the road to success.

Respect gets respect. Disrespect gets disrespect.

What you give, you get. It all ties together. It all comes around in the end. Your choice. And when you start looking at people with respect, starting conversations and asking questions about them and their life and all that, you will be AMAZED at what will be laid in your lap to help you to your dream. I've literally had more deals "find me" just because I was treating someone with respect, talking to them, asking questions, and listening to their answers. This often leads to referrals and suggestions, some have even picked up the phone and made introductions for me to top executives and officials I would have never got to first base with otherwise. People want the secrets to success, and this is one that sounds too simple to believe. But it works.

Where Do Mentors Hang Out?

I've found some great mentors in groups like SCORE (the Service Core of Retired Executives). You can also check out sororities and fraternities; they all have mentoring and tutoring programs. I'm not talking about the current president of the local chapter; I'm talking about all those previous members with their pictures on the wall. I'm talking about old school. Alumni. Past Jedi Masters. So you have all of the previous people who were in there from years before who can take you under their wing. There you go.

Big Brothers and Big Sisters are another good source for mentors, because just to become a big brother they have to have accomplished much in their lives.

A mentor may be someone in your neighborhood whom you admire and want to be like, somebody you've seen but never talked to. There are church and community mentorship and protégé programs in almost every urban area.

100 Black Men, Future Business Leaders of America, Veterans of Foreign Wars, Boys and Girls Clubs—the list goes on and on. You can even do a simple search on Google or MySpace to look for a mentor, and you'll find one pretty fast.

Every success I've had has always been the direct result of a mentor or mentors who've taken an interest in me and opened up new worlds to me.

I've already mentioned one of my earliest mentors, Phillip St. James. He was youth director at a different church than I went to. My youth leader and Phil were good friends, so our two groups did a lot of joint activities together.

Phil started ministering to the youth at his church around the time I was 10. He was around 30 and involved in computer science, so we had a natural connection. We didn't meet until I was probably 12 or so, when I moved up from elementary kids to the youth department. His church had a lot of inner city, at-risk kids, and I was impressed that he always seemed to be patient with them.

Phil taught me a lot, but after he left, he taught me even more by his choices in life. Phil walked away from a successful career in information technology, which was my passion as a teenager, to follow his heart. He got a master's degree in business management, and used it to find ways of marrying corporate wealth with social outreach, through corporately-sponsored social programs. Today he serves as U.S. manager for corporate giving and philanthropy for Sanofi-Aventis, Europe's largest (and the world's third largest) pharmaceutical company, where he specializes in corporate sponsored social and community programs. This commitment on his part was tremendously inspiring to me, and helped shape the course for our companies to become socially conscious in everything we do. As Phil tells it,

Even at a young age, adults could hold an intelligent conversation with Ephren. He listened—rare at any age, especially during teen years—but he also grasped what was being said, and gave intelligent feedback. Ephren actually went out and did the kinds of things I always told my young people to do, but which they mostly never seemed to do. He's always tackled things head-on, never tried to slide by. Even some pretty hard things. And if anyone ever tells him he can't, it's like saying sic 'em to a bulldog.

He just gets it: It's not all about making the money; money's not the main motivation. It's about affecting other peoples' lives. But the money is an important part of achieving that higher goal. And Ephren knows he has to balance both.

In 2006, Phil was the first of my mentors I brought onto the board of City Capital Corporation. He brings an outstanding understanding of the management and logistics requirements of complex operations in an international marketplace, as well as a keen understanding of how to meet the needs of individuals and communities in a cost-effective way, with long-lasting results. Phil has a brilliant mind and a compassionate heart, the kind of combination of business skills and humanitarian passion that define our vision for the company.

Another "sounding board" mentor for me is Darrell McGregor. Darrell used to work for FedEx and has a real handle on customer service and systems, and how to make both work in a win-win way. Darrell met me through Phil, who had told him about the opportunity to invest in a real estate venture. Darrell always had a real heart for our investment strategies for churches. About a year after we met, Darrell took a buy out from FedEx. He asked me "What can I do to help?" and we began traveling together to churches all over the Midwest, speaking and teaching about our community investment programs. It was Darrell who convinced me to move our operations to Franklin, Tennessee, and he was part of our first home office team there, along with Melissa Grimes. Nowadays Darrell does most of our work with churches, while I focus on the public, for-profit side of our business.

Darrell and Phil have helped me keep our company on a high moral course. I get asked a lot of times if City Capital is a "Christian company." And my answer is always the same. I am a Christian, and I've built this company on Godly principles. But a company can't be Christian—or Jewish, or Islamic or any other religious affiliation. A company is made up of people, and if you bring in people of high moral caliber, then the company will grow with a focus on giving back and doing the right things. Darrell has been an important element in reminding me and our staff at times about our origins, and how the work we do today in the for-profit sector is a direct reflection of those values and principles that we started with, working first with churches.

I find people in business that I deal with either get it, or they don't. It's not about the money as much as it is about people. And the people on my team have a heart for the work we do. It goes way beyond just the money.

Other Kinds of Mentors

If there's one particular business that interests you, I recommend you go out and find someone who's currently doing it successfully. For these mentors, I prefer using active business owners and executives because they are right in the moment in the business marketplace you want to be in. I've actually opened up a phone book and started calling companies before, but there are a lot better ways to find a mentor. The best by far is to have an introduction.

Bankers, attorneys, and accountants all have Rolodexes (okay, that's old school: "Contact Files") full of potential mentors, and are usually happy to give a good general reference. In fact, in all situations I always try to remember to ask for a reference for someone who might be able to give some advice and mentoring. Some people will even pick up the phone and call someone to introduce you. I've even had people set up a three-way lunch, so they could provide a personal introduction. It doesn't get much better.

Professional trade associations are another great resource. These exist for every type of career and business interest. Business clubs and civic clubs have all sorts of resources to tap into—Lions, Kiwanis, Rotary, your local merchants' association, Chambers of Commerce. Some of these even have formal mentoring programs, where they help match you up with a mentor, but almost all of them will give you personal references one-on-one if you simply call their offices or attend one of their meetings. You may need to consider membership in the organization, but that's a small price to pay.

Whatever way you can, get introduced to potential mentors. But think of your initial conversation with them as a time to get acquainted, a chance to see if your personalities mesh well, and a little bit of an interview (you are interviewing them to see if they fit your needs). Just remember, you are the one seeking guidance.

Be open and friendly, listen, and don't be too quick to blow off a little hesitation or roughness at first. Iron sharpens iron, and the objective of the first conversation, usually, is just to see if the chemistry is right, and if it is appropriate to set up a longer face-to-face meeting. In most cases, your first contact will be by phone. Great mentors are often busy people, and they don't want to waste time. Occasionally, your first meeting may actually be face-to-face, like with a three-way introduction.

Preparing for Your Face-to-Face

Once you are actually talking with your potential mentor, politely ask him (or her) about his career, his business and if he'd be willing to share his insights with *you* and what are the things he's learned that helped him achieve what he's achieved in his career. Basically, what *he's* found it takes to succeed. Suggest to him that you'd like to take him to lunch, to sit down and talk more about his experiences and outlook, if he's willing.

Just summon up your courage and say, "I'm genuinely wanting to learn about succeeding in business and would really appreciate it if you would be willing to take some time, at your convenience, to talk to me about it. If you'll let me, I'll spring for lunch." Most businesspeople will be flattered and happy to spend a few minutes with you. If there's one thing most people love to do, it's talk about themselves.

More often than not, most of these people are used to picking up the bill at the table. Even though they can easily afford to pay, it's a nice change to have someone offer to buy them lunch for *them*, especially someone who's not trying to sell them something. You don't have to spend a couple hundred bucks, but don't take him to some fast-food joint, either. Take him to a decent restaurant. Better yet, ask him where he'd like to have lunch.

It's a good idea to write up a list of questions beforehand so you'll get the information you really want. Here are some examples of the kinds of questions you might ask when you sit down with them. These aren't in any special order, and you may find there are other pressing questions that aren't listed here. This list will help you get started on your own list. The important thing is, be prepared when you meet with a mentor:

- How did you get into your business?
- What kind of education or training helped you most?
- Who helped you along the way?
- How much money does it take to get started?
- What's the best source for capital for this kind of business?

- What does it takes to be successful?
- What are the hardest things about the business?
- What do you like best about it?
- What do you like least about it?
- What brings you the most customers?
- What organizations do you recommend for people in the business?
- What local organizations have been most useful and beneficial to you?
- What would you do differently if you were starting out today?
- What have been some of your biggest mistakes?
- What was your biggest triumph?
- Where do you see the business going in the future?
- Would you recommend it for someone like me?
- What's the best way for someone to get started in the business today?

If you're fortunate, you will find someone who loves what he does and communicates his enthusiasm to you. This is the kind of person who can inspire you to work hard to achieve a similar level of success and enjoyment.

If, however, the person you talk to is discouraging and negative, listen to what they have to say, but don't let their negativity turn you off. Find another person and get a second point of view (Remember David? *"And he turned from him to another. . . ."*). The more you can pick their brains, the clearer the picture you'll get about the business you're interested in.

Perhaps you'll find out the business isn't all that great. Maybe the market was good a few years back, but conditions have changed. If you meet someone who's negative and unhappy, it may be because his business is going down, or he isn't doing well healthwise, or he just doesn't enjoy the business anymore. Ask him direct questions about what went wrong or why he is so down. The answers could be valuable information that could help you avoid big mistakes in the future.

The most important thing is that you will be talking to people who are active in the business today. You will get a real-world picture of the business, the ins and outs, ups and downs . . . and not some glossed over description from a book.

Follow Up Your Initial Interview

After the interview, be sure to send a handwritten thank you note . . . not an e-mail. Oh, you can e-mail him, too, but the thank you note will be noticed and appreciated more than the email. The next time you see that person, say hello and reintroduce yourself. He may very well remember you, but if his memory fails him you've just given him a polite refresher that will also open a new conversation.

You might even want to find some good reason to revisit with him again, so you can set a tentative second date before your lunch is over. This will keep the contact fresh, and could lead to a greater business relationship. Besides giving you knowledge and insights, a mentor can often provide some valuable introductions. He can open doors to people you'd ordinarily never get in to see.

Usually it's pretty hard to get the chance to ever talk with an average executive or local leader to discuss a business deal, but if an experienced veteran or influential person in the community—like your mentor—recommends you, it's like an instant "Pass Go" to access their network and their world.

Sincerity Goes a Long Way

Think of these relationships almost like a marriage. If you're just going through the motions and have no desire to put an effort into building the relationship, then you're wasting your time and theirs, and it won't help you much in the long-run. That kind of selfishness will show through. You've got to get it fixed in your head that this is going to be win-win for both of you, and make a real effort to make it a valuable relationship all the way around. Apathy, ignorance, and plain laziness will keep you from success and from discovering how very many people in this world see their legacy as a seed that will grow as you become successful.

After all, mentoring you is straight ego for them. Believe me, I've never met a successful person who didn't want to be a mentor and actually make an impact on somebody's life.

Mentors are like diamond mines of information for those who take the time to mine them.

There's a great old book called *Acres of Diamonds* (New York: Fleming H. Revell, 1960). It's just a little book, takes about a half-hour to read. It's from a speech that was given over 6,000 times by Russell Conwell and tells a story of a farmer who sold his farm for pennies on the dollar to run off and search for diamonds. The farmer lost everything and eventually died. One day the buyer was walking around and noticed a black stone in a stream on the property. It had a glint in the sunlight, and he thought it would look good on his mantle. Turns out they were rough diamonds. In fact, the whole farm became the largest diamond mine in the world, the Golconda. Acres and acres of diamonds, and the farmer had ditched it to run off after his fortune.

It's not that farfetched. In 1847 a California man who had caught "gold fever" sold his farm to a Colonel Sutter, who put a mill on the property. Sutter's daughter found some "pretty sand" in the stream, and there at Sutter's Mill the California gold rush began.

Like the diamonds in that farmer's stream, or the gold the California farmer left behind, we have gems of valuable information, knowledge, and experience all around us, just waiting to be picked. Mentors with their knowledge base are more valuable to your company than diamonds, more valuable than a cash investment. What you can learn from them will make you stronger, faster, and better at executing and making key business decisions. With access to their knowledge, it will almost be like having a whole other business plan, one with all the keys of success written in.

Your mentors have been around the block a time or two, a lot farther than you or I have. This has given them incredible business experience, and also dozens of contacts that in the world of business are like money in the bank. In fact, these contacts are worth much more than money, because they can kick open doors when you're trying to start a new business. These connections can help you find the services and individuals that will help you along the way. As you grow, your business mentors can open up access to millions of dollars of capital. They can open up more sources of money you never knew existed.

Ever hear the expression, "It's not what you know, it's *who* you know?" Sometimes people with the right connections have a distinct competitive advantage in the marketplace. The more people you know, the easier it is to get things done, get jobs, and get what you want.

It's all because of their name, and the influence and respect it carries within their business field and their community. No wonder the Bible says a good name is worth more than silver and gold.

> A good name is more desirable than great riches; to be esteemed is better than silver or gold.
>
> —*Proverbs 22:1*

Going out and talking to active businesspeople helps you make valuable mentoring contacts who can open doors and help you in other ways in the future. In every business I've had, mentors have shown me the way. They've cut years off the time it would have taken me to acquire my business knowledge.

In fact, I tell people all the time, if you go into a business, especially if you don't have the experience and this is your first time out, don't even try to make it on your own without a mentor:

> *Believe me, going into an entrepreneurial venture*
> *without a mentor is business suicide.*

Most people really feel like they're obligated somehow to make all the mistakes themselves, to reinvent the wheel when they need one, to tough it out. There's also this pride thing going on: They don't want to be told what to do; they want to go their own way. They're uncomfortable building a team of strong people, and usually it's because their own self-worth or self-esteem gets in the way,—or their ego. Either way, it's a "hard row to hoe," as my great-aunt used to say.

I like easy when I can get it. It is so much easier to find someone who's *been there and done that*, and then actually take his or her advice. Take it in with a filter, sure, but actually listen. The advantage is that you gain years of experience and you don't have to repeat the mistakes that somebody else made. It really is that simple. We all try to make it so difficult with all our, "Yeah, but . . ."

We don't know what we don't know.

It's real easy to think we've got it all figured out. The truth is, a lot of times we don't even know the right questions to ask, to get us the answers we need. For life, business, whatever. Me, I wanted all the help I could get.

I started so young, I couldn't even open up my own checking account for my first company. I had to get my parents to do it for me. But I didn't let what I didn't know—or what I couldn't do by myself—stop me from getting what I needed. And I didn't let my ego or some kind of false pride stop me from bringing in other people and saying, "I need help." I guess you could say when it came to learning what I needed, especially to grow my business, I had no pride.

Because I started so young, I knew there was a lot of stuff I didn't know yet, but I still kind of figured I had a lot of it down. I was real aware that I had to go find the knowledge I needed, but I had no idea how much I didn't know. And guess what? I'm still learning. I guess that's why I still look for mentors.

How I Learned These Things

Most of what I know has come from others who spent years getting beat up and beat down: my mentors. I learned from their lessons. I learned from their successes and failures. Most of what I learned I learned from my mentors. Here's a specific example. When I was in high school I enrolled in the work-study program where you're supposed to go to school half the day and work the other half as an intern. I worked under a mentor named John Vandewalle.

John is from South Africa. A white South African. And here I am this scrawny little black kid from Mississippi. But the relationship I built with him made it possible for me to start my first Internet company when I was in high school. He was the former CEO of Teva Pharmaceuticals and CEO of Clint House, a medical testing company. He was very experienced in business and deal making, taking businesses that weren't performing and turning them around again. So a lot of times I sat right there in his consulting sessions taking notes, like a fly on the wall, soaking it all up like a sponge.

I didn't just go in and punch a clock. I did whatever it took, at whatever hour it was needed, for as long as necessary. I was their go-fer, I did filing, I did a ton of research on other companies, met with the business owners, and a whole lot more. It didn't pay squat, but I got the gold when it came to understanding business.

I worked with this guy for like 60 or 80 hours a week, even worked weekends, for three, maybe four years. My friends all told me I was crazy. Told me I should be charging him, that he was using me. They all went off and found paying jobs, like at the local burger joint. But John had me studying companies that were failing, why they were failing, what it would take to turn them around. So what's my payoff, for all these long hours?

There I was, 14 or 15, right in the middle of this environment with all these successful businesspeople, researching a lot of businesses that were failing. I learned how to run a company and how to put together deals. I learned what makes a company work, and what kills it. When I look at a new venture today, I know all the common mistakes that kill most businesses—we're talking 95 percent or more. And I know a whole bunch of the not-so-common causes, too. I know what to look for, and what to avoid. I know what to do with a bargain-priced company to make it profitable again, using information the current owner doesn't have because they never took the time to seek out a mentor to show them.

Today, I know I can take almost any underperforming asset and make it perform, make it start making money. That's my whole business plan in one sentence. Doesn't matter if it's real estate, oil and gas, technology, you name it. You think that business owner would be bailing if he knew how to turn it around? Of course not. He'd be asking top dollar for his company.

So, instead of taking the long route and hitting a ton of pot-holes and a ton of mistakes, instead of going from Point A to Point Z in 10 years, I can go from A to Z in two years. I buy those existing businesses or assets and make them start producing income for our company today.

Being Accountable

I made myself accountable to John, too, as my mentor, that is. I wasn't just going and getting his advice so I could choose to use it or ignore it if I felt like it. I was working hard and seeking his guidance, and then doing what he said no matter how uncomfortable it felt. It was grueling—a constant learning and development process.

I had no way of knowing how much of this would directly influence my success, learning all the things businesspeople do wrong, or do right in their business. How can someone can be all eat up with excuses about why their business isn't working, and not see the big picture? They would sit there and say it was because of the market, or their staff, or how their competition had saturated the area, or how they just couldn't compete with the big-box stores or the Internet. I heard every excuse under the sun. Then John would bring in our team and we'd turn their losing company into a profitable business and sell it off for more than we paid for it.

I learned all this because I was willing to work long hours and be accountable to him. It all goes back to making a conscious decision. I chose to make myself accountable to John, without pay, so I could learn what he knew.

John would give me some of the information and training one-on-one, then he'd tell me what books to read and send me out to read them. Then the next time we'd talk he'd ask me questions about what I'd learned—sometimes in front of other people. And he expected me to be up on it so I could explain what I'd learned in my own words.

Then I'd ask him more questions. He didn't just give it all to me on a silver platter . . . he made me work for the knowledge and experience I got. If I hadn't, I would have never gotten as much out of it. In fact, the whole experience led me to name one of my companies, "Own the Pond," because of one of his favorite sayings was, "You give a man a fish and you feed him for a day; teach him to fish and you feed him for a lifetime." He fed me and taught me to fish . . . and he gave me the whole pond: the pond of his knowledge, so I have an endless supply of "fish" for the rest of my life.

I do the same thing with our high school and college interns. I look at them as potential mentees. I assign them a whole bunch of books that most "normal" teenagers are not going to read or even want to read. Maybe books like *The One Minute Manager*, by Ken Blanchard, or *Swim with the Sharks*, by Harvey McCay. I have a whole library of business and self-help books.

If they come back to me and have actually started reading them, I know they have the right mindset that says, "I really want to know what you know, and I'll do whatever it takes to get me there."

Anyone can say, "I'll do whatever it takes," but when the rubber meets the road, only one in a hundred actually do. Once I see they have that mindset, I'm able to channel that into patterns of success. I can share with them, by words and example, how to adapt in certain situations, how to look at all the pieces of a puzzle and start fitting them together in your head. Every deal is a puzzle, every business transaction is a completed picture. If even one piece is missing, it's not a complete picture, and with enough pieces out of whack it spoils the whole deal.

Mentors Help Bridge the Gap between Knowledge and Experience

Back in the old days, if a young kid wanted to learn how to make shoes or bake bread, he wouldn't go and read books for years without putting the information to use. He would apprentice to, say, the shoemaker, or the baker. He'd shadow him, and immediately apply everything he learned: his mentor. He learned as he worked, and worked as he learned. He learned by example, by experience, and by application. Sure, he'd make some mistakes, but only small ones because that was all the responsibility he was given at first. Then, as he grew, he was given more and more responsibility. Because he had learned the basics first, he could take on bigger tasks and become successful at his craft. If he started to stumble, his mentor was there . . . sometimes to correct him and sometime letting him fall. Trial and error, trial and success. Learn and do. Do and learn.

Words mean nothing. Action is the only thing. Doing. That's the only thing.

—*Ernest J. Gaines*

It sounds simple, really. But in actual practice it may mean working long hours with no partying, no drinking, and none of the other luxuries a lot of young people feel is their due. Why? For me, I didn't want to repeat the process that my father went through, I didn't want to travel the road that he was still on: working 30 years for somebody else. I saw that there was a shorter path and I was willing to do whatever it took to actually get to my goals faster, within reason. Anything at all to make it work . . . as long as it's legal, moral, and ethical, and proven possible at least once, I'll try it. In fact, that pretty much sums up my criteria to get involved in a business venture even today.

It's about having the willingness to *act*. Not just to *think* about what we know, but to act on the information and move on great deals and great ideas. To act on what we know, immediately, whenever an opportunity arises for us to take action on. To get the information we need, look at it, and then make our decisions quickly.

Applying the Things You Learn

The *application* part of the mentoring process isn't any different from applying any other knowledge, except it's more "real-time." You don't start applying what you've learned after some fixed moment in time. You do it progressively, in bits and pieces as you learn.

You don't sit at the feet of a mentor for 10 years and then go out into the world and make your fortune. You have to do it all *at the same time* you're learning. You take what you learn and run with it. You come back and report and get some course correction and try it again. Meanwhile, you're getting new knowledge, new information, and testing the new ideas out at the same time.

It doesn't have to be million-dollar deals. It doesn't have to be huge, world-class art or hit songs. Do little tests at first, then bigger and bigger. But you keep going forward, you keep on keeping on. Do you think for one second I started out with big deals and big decisions? Of course not. I started out with a decision to make a video game, rather than just whine about not having one. Then I took the steps necessary to make that happen. Then I took what I had made—for myself, mind you—and began to sell it. And began using the knowledge I had gained to make money by doing programming for other companies.

Success seems to be connected with action. Successful men keep moving. They make mistakes, but they don't quit.

—*Conrad Hilton*

Along the way I had to find other mentors and other knowledge, and have other experiences. They built on each other until I could begin incorporating the things I learned at different times from different mentors into my daily actions. As I added, mentor upon mentor, new knowledge on top of knowledge, all the pieces of the puzzle started coming together and working together in new ways.

My knowledge and experience were a combination of all of my mentors, *plus myself and my own talents*. Each of us is made up of many parts, and then one day you realize you are greater than the sum of all those parts. You are more than just a collection of thoughts and ideas. You are synergy in practice. You will eventually outgrow some of your mentors, and their integrity really shows when they tell you that you have outgrown what they can give you.

I *Still* Rely on Mentors

You never stop taking on new mentors; you never stop the learning process. As recently as 2006, I met Harvey Lynch. Harvey was old school, with a tremendous amount of knowledge. He had a radio background that's second to none. He even gave national radio host Tom Joyner his first job. Then he became an international entrepreneur for years, working between America, Africa (including South Africa, Zimbabwe, Swaziland, and others) and Europe (including England, Germany, Belgium, and others). He supplied the oil and gas industry.

Harvey would get pipe from overseas, including Africa and Europe, bring it here to the United States and fabricate it into every imaginable fitting needed for a rig to operate. Everything that went down a hole: Rope, soap, pipe, and fittings. He was one of very few African American business owners in oil and gas, Harvey wanted someone to pass the advantage of his knowledge and experience on to the next generation. He wanted to create a successful young role model to show African Americans and all minorities how they can succeed in the biggest of industries. So he did a search online for "black CEO" and found my name.

Harvey literally took me on as a protégé and said, "I'm going to pass on everything I know about this business to you. I had my opportunity, now you'll have an opportunity; A chance to change the image and raise the vision of African Americans and minorities, to show just how much is possible." After meeting Harvey, I had the same vision.

Harvey sees the big picture, not just how much money can be made. He sees the potential, the reasons bigger than money. He understands that our success will elevate the way thousands of other young people of all races view their abilities and dreams. He gets it. Here's how he puts it:

> *Ephren provides exactly the kind of positive image today's young and aspiring African Americans so desperately need. As another of my protégés, Tom Joyner recognized, Ephren Taylor is truly* living black history. *From his technological savvy, to his incredible business and deal-making acumen, to his dynamically innovative productivity incentive plans, Ephren is truly a history maker.*

We created a new City Capital subsidiary called Goshen Energy. Then, much like in purchasing distressed real estate, Harvey helped me find our first natural gas deal: A floating rig in the Gulf of Mexico that had been damaged by Hurricane Katrina in 2004. A producing gas well with $48 million in certified reserves. Eight billion cubic feet of natural gas reserves. Eight billion . . . I love saying that. And all we had to do to get it up to full production was to buy a new compressor because the old one was worn out. It just didn't pull enough gas out to make the well profitable any more, and the group of investors wanted to cash out instead of rehabbing the pump and platform and bringing it up to speed.

We bought an oil well, too, with estimated crude oil reserves of 600,000 barrels. It's figured to be worth around $38 million. Unbelievable. By the way, using the knowledge from other mentors along the way, I didn't have to write a check out of my wallet for these investments. Through a combination of money from investors and stock, the transaction was put together almost overnight.

But my mentor had already opened doors to something even bigger: biofuels. Almost as quickly as we had gotten into pumping oil and gas, we got out of that area of energy and began focusing on developing biofuels.

Most people have heard of ethanol, which is usually made from corn or soybeans, but there are thousands of other crops that produce much more oil per acre than these crops, and they don't cut into the food market. Even though there's a big push for more ethanol, while writing this book news reports have focused on how taking more acres of food crops is driving up prices on other things, like eggs and meat, that depend on these crops, too.

We started finding communities that were rolling out the red carpet for City Capital to bring in Goshen Energy and produce biodiesel and other fuels. It was just like in real estate, where the cities needed affordable housing. Everyone needs affordable fuel, and renewable fuels give us an environmentally-sound way to fill this need. It also helps us loosen the grip of foreign oil, and everyone wants to see us less dependent on these other nations.

State representatives began calling me, even leaders of other nations, offering the necessary land and other incentives. I realized this opportunity was the future I'd dreamed of for our company. I began looking at many of the real estate projects and seeing the time and effort to provide even a few houses. When I compared this to the relative ease of creating an operation that could keep millions of gallons of waste oil and millions of tons of solid waste out of landfills, and create an ongoing production for long-term revenues for Goshen and City Capital, there was no contest. I decided to find and re-channel our efforts to putting together the deals and alliances with cities, and finding real estate partners to take over the physical development of properties. This way, we could put most of our focus on developing biofuels nationwide.

As of the time this book was completed, I have almost completed this transition for City Capital. We are already entering the new field of bio energy and hope to make this our main focus within the next year.

Needless to say, finding mentors like Harvey Lynch can change your entire outlook and business destiny. While Harvey went looking for me, most of the mentors we've mentioned have been ones that you might meet casually, or people who are all around you just waiting to be asked. But if you don't take the time to look, and don't approach them from a giving, win-win position, you won't find the ones who have the knowledge and experience you need to succeed.

The Ultimate Legacy: Immortality

You see, mentors see the possibility of their biggest dream coming true through you: immortality. Okay, nothing can really make us immortal, but this is about as close as it gets: You become their legacy.

Like I shared earlier, their kids and family don't know their value and probably don't care. They may love them as their father or mother, sister or brother, aunt or uncle. But they don't know them nearly as intimately as you have come to know them. They have passed on their life knowledge to you. Can you see why mentoring is so powerful? With real mentors, it's not about getting something from you, some hidden agenda, "what's it worth to you?" It's about passing on the torch, seeing that their knowledge won't die when they do.

That's why true mentors won't hold back, they'll give you everything they've got. It's also why they're so tough on you. They won't take your trash talk and they don't believe your excuses. They'll turn their back on you in a minute, if they think you're not sincere and just wasting their time, and not really willing to run the race. They're in this whole thing because they want to back a champion, not a wannabe.

All you have to do is want to be a champion,
A winner, and a success in life. Do you?

If so, find yourself a mentor, build the relationship, and do whatever it takes. Apply the knowledge you learn. You will make mistakes, you will have some really difficult experiences, but *nothing* compared to going it alone because you don't know what you don't know. As I said in the beginning of this section, to me, doing business without mentors is suicidal. They've been there, done that, and they've already gotten and given away or burned more T-shirts in the process than you've ever owned. Do whatever it takes to find the mentors you need.

SECTION VII

Don't Listen to Losers, Whiners, and
Naysayers—Believe in Yourself

'd be lying if I led you to believe that everything I have ever done was easy and that there were never any problems. No matter what you set out to do there will be obstacles. Worse yet, there will be no end to the crowds of people who will try to bring you down. Whether it is from misguided love, envy, or pure meanness they will argue that everything you're doing is wrong.

They can be your best friends, your parents, your spouse, your school buddies, even your own employees. These people automatically assume they have a better answer than you do. Usually their advice is to simply not do whatever it is you're planning. They will tell you the timing is wrong, the location is bad, the name sucks, the logo is awful, the product is wrong, and that nobody will buy what you're selling.

If you have any self doubts at all, these individuals will zero right in on them. They'll jump up and down on your dreams and kick your well-laid plans all over the parking lot. No matter how difficult it is, you must learn to tune them out or keep them out. No matter how well meaning they profess to be, their negativity will only do you harm.

There are two things to keep in mind when the naysayers start yapping. The first has to do with their *qualifications*. Ask yourself these questions about their free advice:

- Have any one of these people actually done anything even close to what you want to do?
- Do they have any first hand experience?
- Are they experts in the exact area that you're entering?

Ninety-nine percent of the time the answer will be no. They are usually the kind of know-it-alls who have only superficial knowledge and they think it qualifies them as experts who can give you personal advice.

Unless someone has impeccable credentials and unquestioned expertise in the specific area your business covers, their advice is practically worthless. Even if they have done something that's almost but not quite the same, what they have to say is not that important.

The second set of questions may be even more important. These have to do with their *objectives:*

- Where are they coming from?
- What is behind their advice? A spouse may tell you not to take risks because you are part of his or her financial support. They have a vested interest in keeping things the same. Unfortunately, you can never move ahead if you never take that chance, and chances are, you won't be very happy doing the same old-same old. You may need to tell your spouse that you need him or her to trust you and support you in your quest for your dreams.
- Do they have another agenda? Would they benefit somehow from you not entering the business, or if you failed? Friends who have never had any success may not want you to have any either. Although they would never say so, deep down inside they want to keep you down where they are. That would keep their world the way they like it.

Realize that these agendas may not all have to do with money. They can also be emotional. Some people have a fixed image of you. They see you as the guy or girl who just goes to school or goes to work and never does anything out of the ordinary. They don't know your true potential so they may say that you're not cut out to be a businessperson. Just like the teacher who said Thomas Edison was addled, they don't have an inkling about what you are capable of. And that person we talked about earlier, the potential mentor who's similar business had failed, he has an agenda, too. Out of a real concern, they may not want you to have the same fate. They may urge you not to go into this new venture because you could end up like they did. Or, they could feel you may succeed, and their excuses for failure would be invalidated. All you can say to them is—that was then and this is now. You are a different person with a different plan and their failure does not mean that you will fail.

There isn't an entrepreneur on the planet who hasn't had to wade through oceans of naysayers in order to achieve what he or she set out to do. The problem these people present is that they can divert your attention from your goal. They can shake your self-confidence. They can make you start to second-guess yourself and to doubt the validity of your dream, which is not productive.

The danger is, you might start to listen to some of these losers and whiners and you might take what they say to heart. You can already see what will result from that, I don't even have to tell you. It's not pretty. Two things will keep this from happening: *firmness* and *focus*.

For me, it's a lot easier to be firm with friends and relatives (and others) who criticize or ridicule what I'm trying to do. It has been this way my whole life. This goes back to my David example; just brush it off and go find someone else to give you feedback. Some people find the slightest criticism shuts them down. They can't handle what they see as rejection. Deal with it. Expect it. Welcome it. You will suffer rejection, and most of the time you'll never know what's really behind it (that's why I gave you the questions above, to help sort some of this out).

It's more difficult to be firm with those you love and care for, and who love and care for you, when their concern is for your well-being. Often their advice will fall in "the higher you go the harder you'll fall" category, but hear them out anyway, because they may have some points worth paying attention to. They deserve that much, at least.

Just don't subject yourself to endless discussions where they're trying to convince you to go against your dream, your goal, your vision. These can easily spiral down into extremely negative sessions, with not-so-gentle reminders of past failures thrown in. Being firm here is vital. You have to be hard, hold up your hand and stop it before it starts. You have to learn to shake yourself up, get serious and tell your friends and relatives that if they truly care about you, they won't subject you to negativity and criticism. Appreciate their concern, and if they have specific points or suggestions, respect them enough to hear them out. But make it clear that you are determined to succeed and stick to your guns.

Focus. That's where you'll find your strength to persevere. Focusing on your goal. Keep in mind what we talked about earlier: it must be real. You must live it, breathe it, and feel it. It's already real, just waiting for you to catch up. It's yours. You don't have to stomp all over people, or be a hater or hurter to reach it. You don't have to be a jerk or do illegal or immoral things. Focus is the element that renews your strength and keeps the big picture alive, in the midst of all the little crises and fires and potholes along the way.

Maintaining your focus isn't always easy. Dealing with the starts and stops along the way, the difficulties and roadblocks, all takes focus, and keeping the faith during these difficult times is a real brain drain. Be prepared to physically and emotionally put it all on the line for your goal, and believe in your dream.

Sometimes, it may even come down to avoiding some people you know and love. It's sad to say, but as you move up in the world, you may leave behind some of the people who are not moving up, or who don't want to because of their own fears and excuses. You can lead them by your example, but as the old saying goes, you can't push a rope. The ones that are true will still love you and care for you. Your real friends won't be angry or resentful, and in the end will accept your decisions and celebrate your successes with you. The ones who can't are showing their true colors, and a lot of times, it may hurt. But the choice is really theirs. You've made your choice, to go for your goal. You've found that true success was always inside you, and you've created the successes in your life from the inside out.

Epilogue: Dream Bigger Dreams

One of my mentors once told me the story of Ted Turner and Turner Broadcasting. When Ted's father died, he left him a couple of million dollars and this advice: "Dream bigger dreams than you can achieve in your lifetime." As I've shared in this book, I believe that personal success for selfish reasons is no success at all. True success builds lives, families, and communities. True success gives back and gives a leg up for others. True success leaves a legacy of positive change, of giving, not just getting.

When you dream, make them big ones! One of the things I've appreciated about Emerson Brantley, who helped me to get this book done, was that he wasn't blown away by my vision. In fact, he saw it as something even bigger. He saw it as big as I really wanted it to be, but I had scaled it down after years of being told my dream was too big. I wanted to build a multimillion-dollar company, but Emerson told me I'd be wasting my time if I wasn't going for a minimum $100 million dollar company—or more. I planned to build it up and sell it as a private company. Those usually get 3 to 5 times earnings. He said why not take it public, and get several times that? I'd always wanted to take a company public, but along the way, we all face the danger of letting the day-to-day battles of running a business lower our expectations, if we're not careful.

Your Dreams Aren't Big Enough!

Most people self-limit their dreams. If you think your dreams are pretty big, make them even bigger. If you want 1,000 customers a year for your first year, go for 10,000. Or 100,000. I'm not talking about pipe dreams. I'm talking about a mindset. If you plan for super-success, odds are you'll be further ahead at the end of the year than planning for just enough to get by. Or like the old saying goes:

> *It's better to aim for the stars and hit the moon,*
> *than aim for the moon and hit the barn.*

You really don't know *what you don't know*. You don't know that you can't accomplish what you want. You don't know that you can't raise the capital you need. You don't know that you can't dominate your market. Why assume that you know when you don't? Why limit yourself to the conservative projections of what you can do and how much you can grow? Go for it!

Conservative projections are only good for figuring breakeven points, nothing more. And on the profit/loss sheet, breaking even is just that: Zero. It's the point where you've covered your costs—but still haven't made any money. It's the best of the worst, and the worst of the best. And it's average. You are so much more than average. You have the seeds of success already, right inside you. The only real limitations are the ones you accept.

You may remember me saying there are more dollars than deals out there. Part of the reason for this Emerson explained was that most people feel beat down when they talk to bankers and friends about their deal. They whittle their business plan down to "just enough to get buy." The trouble is, by lowering their goals, they shoot themselves in the foot. Serious lenders look at their "conservative" numbers and figure they aren't thinking far enough ahead. They just want a mediocre business. What will happen if something throws a wrench in the works? Where's the ability to get through Murphy's Law moments and hard times? Where's the reserve capital for a "rainy day" or unforeseen difficulties?

So even the lenders want to see big dreams. If you need a million, ask for 5, or 10. And show them in your plan how you'll use it to expand your business. (*Hint:* Not by bumping your salary!) Show them that you have a vision and a plan.

What Do You Want?

Your vision and dreams for your business are important, but what business plan do you have for your relationships, your marriage, your family? What plan do you have for giving to others, for "paying it forward?" Think big, then bigger, with these goals, too. I plan on doing a lot more missions to Africa, but not just to drop off some medical supplies. I want to change villages and whole countries. I want to bring biofuels to these countries and provide fuel and other resources so the citizens can be self-sufficient. From discussions we're already having, I've already had to make my dream bigger! Now we're looking at huge farms, providing jobs for hundreds of people, and using the byproduct of our biofuel production for local farmers as fodder for their animals and fertilizer for their family farms.

I intend to continue working with even more cities, states, and countries. I intend to use my own God-given gifts and success to create deals where villages can be self-sufficient, where families aren't dependent on their cow or their parched cropland to survive. Where men don't have to leave families for a year at a stretch, to work on the oil rigs or diamond mines. I have HUGE dreams. What are yours? Don't be afraid to make them even bigger!

I Started Dreaming Long before I Was Wealthy or Successful

Open your mind and let it go. Trust yourself, and believe in yourself. Play "What if?" for your life, and write down the things you come up with. Dreams are free . . . you don't have to figure out all the details to make them happen. Once you get a handle on what you really want in your life, then begin taking the steps we've talked about in this book. Prioritize them, evaluate them, put timelines on them, and start taking the first steps. Face the fears, drop the excuses, and start enjoying stepping out of your comfort zone. Find mentors. It's never too soon, you can't be too young or too old to start this way. It's your life and your dreams—go for them!

So I leave you with these words: determine within yourself to find the greatness inside you, and navigate through whatever comes along in your life until you find that success, and use it to change lives around you. Dream big dreams. And put legs and feet under them so they can run. Be the leader future generations will look up to. Build a legacy that will outlive you. Dream—and live—big dreams. And you will find true success that comes only from the inside out.

About Ephren W. Taylor II

Born July 17, 1982, Ephren Taylor is one of the youngest CEOs of any public company. He is also *the* youngest African American CEO of *any* public company, ever. And yet, his business experience already spans over a decade of successful ventures. He has started and successfully raised millions in investment capital for several successful companies, partnering with corporate giants including Citigroup, Sprint, Target, and Wal-Mart to create workable programs with impressive results. He has become known as a real estate "Market Maker," a "Wealth Engineer," and in economic development circles a high-performance visionary with the ability to make things happen, when nobody else can.

Business Visionary and Innovator

He started his first successful company, Flame Software, developing 3D video games at age 12. At 16, Ephren won Microsoft's Teen TechFest Challenge, and using $1,000 savings he started a job search engine for teens. A scholarship from the Kauffman Center for Entrepreneurial Leadership built his business skills. He personally raised over $250,000 in angel financing and the company grew into highly successful GoFerretGo.com, ranked by *YoungBiz* magazine as number 4 of the "100 Top Companies Run by Teens" nationwide with a value of $3.4 million dollars.

Retiring from business at age 17, Ephren began a faith-based initiative teaching church members investing and stewardship and assisting congregations in investments that created dramatic returns. His unique outside-the-box approaches turned traditional real estate investing upside-down. He realized real estate was an incredible vehicle for corporate ROI that could also restore value and hope into communities.

Socially-Conscious Investing to Empower Urban Communities

The investment concepts he developed earned him the coveted Kansas Entrepreneur of the Year award in 2002 from the State of Kansas Department of Commerce. The model led to the founding of Amoro Management Group, LLC, and are still used today by City Capital Corporation (STOCK SYMBOL:CCCN). Today, city, state, federal, and even international governments actively seek him out to spearhead vast development and redevelopment projects, often participating as partners.

City Capital Corporation was originally founded in 1984. In 2006, the company asked Mr. Taylor to take the helm as CEO. City Capital is publicly owned with a diversified portfolio of real estate developments in several states, producing oil and gas reserves and an active biofuels program. Christian Capital Group, LLC continues to help churches meet long-term funding needs with real estate and other high-return investments.

City Capital leverages its investments, holdings, and other assets to build value for investors and shareholders, while initiating positive changes in communities nationwide. In real estate, the company partners with cities to create affordable homes for working-class families. The company's unique "Credit-Investor" program even allows individuals to use their credit alone to invest in these homes, for themselves or their favorite charity, with no cash out of their own pocket.

In 2007, City Capital expanded into the buying, selling, and drilling of oil and gas properties and mineral leases, with the acquisition of a Dallas-based group with over 100 years experience. The new company became Goshen Energy Resources, Inc., and began acquiring distressed, but productive properties in the Gulf Coast region.

Team Builder

Although he is a visionary, Ephren Taylor is no maverick. A major part of his success is his insistence on building a unified team of quality, high-performance people, many who are experts in their field. This team includes marketing, communication, banking and finance, real estate development, and construction—over 225 years of experience. These combined strengths give Mr. Taylor valuable insights into the myriad of decisions facing any CEO and allow City Capital to focus on the specific projects that earn the most revenue for investors.

Speaker and Leader

Recognized as an extraordinary young entrepreneur with a unique understanding of our current business marketplace, Taylor has been featured by the Associated Press, the *Wall Street Journal, Boston Globe, Dallas Morning News*, Forbes.com, NAACP The Crisis, Microsoft.com, *Ingrams*, Entrepreneur.com, *Kansas City Star*, *Pitch*, and hundreds of other print and online publications.

He has served as keynote speaker for dozens of colleges and business organizations; as frequent guest panelist for events such as the Wall Street Economic Summit and the Congressional Black Caucus; as industry commentator on hundreds of local and national television and radio shows including CNBC's *Big Idea*, FOX News' *Your World with Neil Cavuto*, and *Bulls and Bears*, the *Tom Joyner Morning Show*, and the *Doug Banks Morning Show*. He currently hosts *The Soul of Success* on Family Talk 170XM on XM Satellite Radio with co-host Emerson Brantley.

Ephren Taylor is also in demand as a speaker for colleges, high schools, churches, and business events, where he encourages audiences young and old to take the necessary steps to reach success in their own lives, as well as in their houses of worship, schools, civic organizations, and communities. His "Urban Wealth Tour" plans to reach 15 cities in 2007 and 2008, promoting economic empowerment, affordable housing, and entrepreneurship in urban communities. Taylor speaks at local high schools, addresses private investors, educators, nonprofit organizations, religious and government leaders to encourage positive change in their urban communities.

Ephren W. Taylor II Timeline

2007

- Goshen Energy Resources announces move into biofuels production.
- Speaks at White House on sixth anniversary of 9/11 attack.
- City Capital announces sale of real estate division to place more focus on renewable energy initiative.
- CNBC begins documentary on Taylor's life to air fall 2007.
- Purchases controlling interest in West Delta gas well, forms Goshen Energy Resources, Inc. as wholly-owned subsidiary of City Capital Corporation.
- Establishes the Ephren W. Taylor II Entrepreneurship Academy at Cheyney University, the oldest black institute of higher learning in America. Taylor's donation, given through the Tom Joyner Foundation, is the largest gift ever received by the 170-year old college.
- Begins Urban Wealth Tour, visiting 15 cities speaking on financial empowerment and affordable housing. Meetings with city, clergy, and community leaders establishing new relationships nationwide.
- Starts national weekly radio show, *The Soul of Success*, on Satellite radio Family Talk XM 170.
- Establishes Credit-Investor Program nationwide, allowing private individuals to invest in urban communities using only their credit.

- Featured panelist, 2007 Wall Street Economic Summit.
- Featured as market commentator on various national news programs including Fox *Your World with Neil Cavuto* and *Bulls and Bears*, and CNBC's *Big Idea* panel.
- City Capital drops its BDC status to allow for quantum growth.

2006

- City Capital closes on Kansas City Historic Jazz District properties, becoming largest single landowner in this historic area. Within two weeks, first sales are posted of the newly acquired properties.
- City Capital Corporation, a business development company (BDC) dating back to 1984, asks Taylor to take over as chairman and CEO. Taylor is 23 years old, the youngest African American CEO of any public company in history.
- Featured Panelist, 2006 Congressional Black Caucus Annual Legislative Convention: "One Block at a Time: Urban Revitalization."
- "Excellence in Business Award," 14th Annual Malcolm X Festival Honoree.
- "Excellent Business Award, 2006," Congresswoman Diane Watson (CA).
- Appoints Melissa Grimes Chief Operating Officer, at 26 the youngest African American female in the COO position in any public company.
- Amoro completes merger with publicly owned Upside Development, Taylor becomes chairman and CEO of new company, named AmoroCorp.
- Forms Amoro Entertainment.
- Invited to speak to college business schools on entrepreneurship, including Cheyney, Spelman, and more.
- Letter of Intent signed for Peregrine Falcon subdivision, first major project with a city partner.
- City of Los Angeles Achievement Award for Outstanding Citizenship and Activities Enhancing Community Betterment.

- Amoro begins managing football league endowment for entertainer Snoop Dogg.

2005

- Forms Amoro Management to manage property acquisitions and development with cities and becomes CEO.
- Forms Amoro Financial to handle mortgage loan brokering and processing and becomes chairmen.
- Approached by major national bank to take over Kansas City Historic Jazz District renovation. This is company's first major scattered-site urban development.
- Ephren Capital formed to pursue larger city and state development projects.

2003

- Founded Christian Capital Group, LLC, to expand from working only with congregations into general investing and development of properties, using Taylor's unique investment concepts. Taylor is CEO.

2001

- iNTouch Connections. Manages IT consulting division with 30 developers and IT consultants. Clients ranged from large pharmaceutical and insurance companies to small businesses. Continues operations for two years, before changing focus from IT development to investing.

2002

- COC Ventures formed to assist other churches in their stewardship, donation and endowment programs, investing in local community properties to provide affordable housing and higher returns on investment. Taylor is CEO.
- Awarded Kansas Youth Entrepreneur of the Year for his exceptional investment concepts which he originally created for churches.

- Johnson County Church of Christ, Assistant Minister (2002 to present). Helped to grow church membership and assisted in acquiring their building. Began working with church investments and developing strategies to help them earn higher returns by investing within the local community, in real estate.
- Kansas University/Wichita State University, Graduate, Mini MBA Program.
- Microsoft Certified Professional, Systems Engineer, Systems Administrator (Charter Member).

2001

- *YoungBiz* magazine ranked GoFerretGo #4 of "100 Top Companies Run by Teens" with a $3.4 million market value.

2000

- Winner, Microsoft "Top Teens in Technology," Teen Tech Fest.

1999

- 4Teens Network (later changed to GoFerretGo, LLC), a job search site for teens and college students, begun with a high school friend. Taylor, age 17 wrote the business plan, managed marketing, web site, call center, and sales team. After his partner left for college, Ephren raised $250,000 as chairman.
- Future Business Leaders of America, National Champion.
- Future Business Leaders of America, State Champion.
- Entreprep Scholarship winner, Kauffman Foundation.

1994–1998

- Flame Software. Age 12, Middle School, where Ephren created and sold a 3D video game and a Windows Notepad replacement program; developed software for a top worldwide nutritional supplement company; and beta tested the Microsoft Gex video game project.

For more ideas on Creating Success from the Inside Out, other books by Ephren Taylor, or to join in discussions about entrepreneurship and success, visit www.createthesuccess.com.

For updates on entrepreneurship training, including online courses, visit Ephrenuniversity.com.

For more information on City Capital Corporation (stock symbol CCCN) visit www.citycapcorp.com.

About W. Emerson Brantley III

In his role as board member and chief communications officer for City Capital Corporation, Emerson Brantley draws on over 30 years experience and national success in marketing and business funding. His expertise as a communicator, marketing professional, and media strategist have been key factors in the company's growing visibility and positive image nationwide.

Serving on the senior management team for a publishing and training firm, his marketing campaigns propelled the company through 1500 percent growth, two listings on the *Inc. 500* list of fastest growing corporations, a successful merger, and a $60 million IPO.

As CEO of Web3Direct.com, a private business consulting and coaching firm, Mr. Brantley has enabled companies in the United States and internationally to target and maximize their marketing efforts, and helped growing companies find business funding to fuel their growth. Considered among the top fifty direct response copywriters in the country, Brantley has masterminded thousands of successful print, mail, online, radio, and television campaigns, including the longest-running lead-generating television infomercial ever aired, generating millions in sales nationwide for the "Cash Flow Generator" real estate course.

A long list of diverse corporations have benefited from Mr. Brantley's marketing and growth strategies. Among his past clients are transportation giant Fruehauf Corporation, global shipping innovator Emery Worldwide, industrial coatings manufacturer Bronz-Glow, real estate seminar and training trendsetter International Media

Holdings, America's oldest nonprofit conservation organization American Forests, and many more. Additionally, he has completed projects for the national offices of Veterans of Foreign Wars, the Baseball Hall of Fame, the Wright Brothers Memorial at Kitty Hawk, and Disney's Epcot Center.

Brantley also serves on the board of an international funding group in the United Kingdom. His network of funding sources has provided City Capital with access to a number of important funding partners. He has refined and targeted the company's existing client base to maximize profits and distilled City Capital's unique positioning statement of "Socially-Conscious Investing to Empower Communities." His development of the company's Credit-Investor Program, including its successful national marketing launch, has brought in hundreds of new qualified investors. As City Capital expands and diversifies operations globally, Brantley's guidance through the quantum growth process, combined with his in-depth business understanding are keys to helping ensure the company's long-term success.

Mr. Brantley received his Bachelor of Arts degree, magna cum laude, from Florida State University in 1976, and holds international professional listings in Who's Who of Business Leaders Worldwide and Certified Marketing Executives. He has served on many civic, business, and nonprofit boards, including being past president of Sales and Marketing Executives.

Mr. Brantley has written or coauthored several business books and courses: *The Cash-Flow Generator, The Maxims of Marketing, Internet Profits Now, How It Gets Done, 21 Secrets of Real Estate Millionaires, Guerilla Marketing for Real Estate Investors,* and the *Mega Mortgage Marketing Seminar,* as well as many other courses, special reports, manuals, sales pieces, and guest feature articles in national publications.

Index